Top 25 locator map
(continues on inside
back cover)
←

D1146955

TwinPack
Lanzarote &
Fuerteventura

ANDREW SANGER

Andrew Sanger is a well-
established travel journalist
who has contributed to a wide
range of popular magazines
and most British newspapers.
He is the author of more than
twenty travel guides, including
Essential Lanzarote, *Essential
Tenerife, TwinPack Tenerife*
and *Explorer Israel* for the AA.
He has twice won at the
annual Travalex Travel Writers'
Awards.

ou have any comments
uggestions for this guide
an contact the editor at
cks@theAA.com

AA Publishing
Find out more about AA Publishing and
the wide range of services the AA provides
by visiting our website at *www.theAA.com*

Contents

About this book

KEY TO SYMBOLS

✚ Grid reference to the Top 25 locator map

⊠ Address

☎ Telephone number

🕓 Opening/closing times

🍴 Restaurant or café on premises or near by

Ⓜ Nearest underground (tube) station

🚊 Nearest railway station

🚌 Nearest bus route

⛴ Nearest riverboat or ferry stop

♿ Facilities for visitors with disabilities

✋ Admission charge

⬌ Other nearby places of interest

❓ Tours, lectures or special events

➤ Indicates the page where you will find a fuller description

ℹ Tourist information

TwinPack Lanzarote is divided into six sections. It includes:

- The author's view of the island and its people
- Suggested walks and excursions
- The Top 25 sights to visit
- The Best of the rest; what makes the islands special
- Detailed listings of restaurants, hotels, shops and nightlife
- Practical information

In addition, easy-to-read side panels provide fascinating extra facts and snippets, highlights of places to visit and invaluable practical advice.

CROSS-REFERENCES

To help you make the most of your visit, cross-references, indicated by ➤ show you where to find additional information about a place or subject.

MAPS

The fold-out map in the wallet at the back of the book is a large-scale island map of Lanzarote.
The Top 25 Locator maps found on the inside front and back covers of the book itself are for quick reference. They show the Top 25 Sights, described on pages 24–48, which are clearly plotted by number (**1** – **25**, not page number) in alphabetical order.

PRICES

Where appropriate, an indication of the cost of an establishment is given by £ signs: £££ denotes higher prices, ££ denotes average prices, while £ denotes lower charges.

LANZAROTE & FUERTEVENTURA
Island life

A Personal View

A clump of pretty orange flowers growing amongst the dark, rocky volcanic landscape

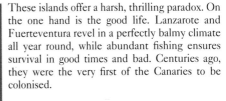

Lichen thrives in the volcanic ash of Montaña de las Lapas o del Cuervo (Parque Nacional de Timanfaya)

These islands offer a harsh, thrilling paradox. On the one hand is the good life. Lanzarote and Fuerteventura revel in a perfectly balmy climate all year round, while abundant fishing ensures survival in good times and bad. Centuries ago, they were the very first of the Canaries to be colonised.

At the same time, Lanzarote and Fuerteventura seem to defy human beings to make a home here. In spirit as well as in distance, these two volcanic islands are close to the Sahara. Harsh, dry, barren, they possess an austere, timeless emptiness, an overwhelming solitude and silence. And, too, there is sometimes an almost menacing hint of Nature's enduring power. Fuerteventura's vast areas of sand grow with every wind from the east. On Lanzarote, the Timanfaya volcano still simmers and smoulders just beneath the surface. Nearly a third of the island is black volcanic *malpais*, which looks impossible to walk on, let alone cultivate.

Yet people came, and settled. First to arrive were the ancient Guanches, who probably sailed in simple reed craft from North Africa. A succession of other peoples came to explore, culminating in the Spanish conquest.

However, the two islands remain thinly populated. Fuerteventura's average of 28 people per sqaure mile is the lowest in all the Canaries, and even that figure gives no clue to the actual sense of space, for almost all the island's populace in fact lives in just one place – the capital, Puerto del Rosario. Lanzarote's case, though not so extreme, is similar: most people are in Arrecife, and most of the countryside offers a vast, sunlit tranquillity. Even those who live in the villages generally work in the capital.

Yet these are not desert islands after all, but Spanish territories with agriculture and art, history, traditions and folklore, a culture and cuisine. Those dauntless settlers and colonists proved that it was indeed possible to do something with the *malpais*, parts of which are now cultivated with the most extraordinary looking vineyards. Each bush sits in its own walled, horseshoe-shaped hollow, and produces a delicious wine. Black pebbles of volcanic stone, it was soon discovered, hold the dew and keep the earth moist. So these were used to cover the fields of this waterless island, making farming possible.

Traditional basket-weaving in Bodega Santa Maria, Bentancuria

And in modern times, they have even become holiday lands with hotels and beaches and satellite TV and cars for hire. That is the paradox – and one which fascinated Lanzarote's influential artist, César Manrique. The unimaginable destructive forces of nature, like the Timanfaya volcano which rained burning rock over Lanzarote and swept away fields and villages which islanders had nurtured for centuries, have themselves now been harnessed by man's own great powers of survival and imagination.

A Monarch butterfly

Getting visitors to pay to see the volcano, and using the Fire Mountain's heat to barbecue steaks, is surely a victory of sorts. A temporary one, perhaps, for Lanzarote and Fuerteventura will outlive us. The volcanoes will erupt again one day, and the sands will continue to blow from Africa.

An awe-inspiring sunset viewed from the main beach of Puerto del Carmen

Lanzarote in Figures

PEOPLE

- Some 65,000 people live on Lanzarote and about 30,000 on Fuerteventura.
- On both islands, well over half the population live in their respective capital.
- Ethnically the islanders are thought to be a mix of Berber, Arab, Norman and Spanish.
- Fuerteventura natives are known as *maioreros*, while Lanzeroteños are called *conejos*, meaning rabbits.

CLIMATE

- Unlike the other Canaries, these two islands remain practically rainfree all year round, though there can be winter cloud. Any rain that does fall normally comes between December and February, and falls on an average of only 16 days per year, with a total annual precipitation of only about 138mm.
- Average daytime temperatures remain almost constant at around 20°C on Lanzarote, 19°C on Fuerteventura all year round.
- Both islands can be windy, especially on the western sides.

SIZE

- The second largest of the Canaries, Fuerteventura is only slightly smaller than Tenerife. At 1,731sq km, it is over twice the size of Lanzarote's 813sq km.

LANGUAGE

- Spanish is the language of the Canaries, but islanders also have a patois of their own. English is widely spoken (though not usually very well), especially in resorts and tourist attractions.

LANDSCAPE

- The volcanic eruptions of the 18th century have left an incredible lunar-like landscape on Lanzarote.
- Notable eruptions of Mount Tiede have occurred in 1462 (as Columbus sailed past), 1604, 1605, 1704–5, 1706, 1798 and 1909.
- Fuerteventura is almost barren, with an unspectacular landscape, due to more than 20 million years of erosion and weathering.

Famous of Lanzarote

César Manrique

César Manrique (1919–92) was born in Arrecife and made Lanzarote famous. The local lad, whose genius made him an international figure in the world of modern art, actually left Lanzarote as a young man. He prospered in New York, Paris and Madrid, formed close friendships with his compatriots Picasso and Miró, and became an acclaimed modern artist.

He eventually returned home in 1968 to a hero's welcome. Manrique adored the island, and was fascinated by man's relationship with landscape. He was also intrigued by the mass tourism then taking off in the Canaries – its destructive power, and equally, the benefits it could bring. Manrique was eager to ensure that development took place with respect for local culture and tradition.

The regional council gave him a free hand to do whatever he wanted, and Lanzarote became Manrique's atelier. He laid down autocratic architectural rules. He banned all roadside billboards (take a look, there aren't any). He put up fantastic, wind-driven giant mobile sculptures at major crossroads. He took over Lanzarote's geographical oddities and with sheer brilliance turned them into extraordinary attractions.

Many of his ideas became law, including the rules that no new buildings may be more than two storeys (except in Arrecife and tourist zones) high, and that window shutters must be plain wood or green, except by the sea, where blue is allowed. While new coastal developments disregard some rules, there are still no high-rise hotels.

In 1978 Manrique received the World Ecology and Tourism Award, and in 1986 the Europa Nostra Award for conservation. In 1992, at the age of 74, César Manrique died in a car crash at the intersection near his home (which he had said for years was dangerous). He is buried at Haría, and today is regarded by the islanders almost in the light of a secular saint.

FAMOUS VISITORS

King Hussein of Jordan once owned a holiday home on Lanzarote (since given to King Juan Carlos I of Spain). Taken to visit Manrique, King Hussein lit up a cigarette, Manrique asked him not to smoke, adding 'In this house, I am the king'.

Raquel Welch, dressed only in a fur bikini, can be seen in a desolate Timanfaya landscape in the film *One Million Years BC*.

Fuerteventura's most distinguished visitor was the poet and philosopher Unamuno, who was exiled here in 1924.

A golden roadside mobile by César Manrique

A Chronology

17–20 million years ago	Huge volcanic eruptions create Fuerteventura and Lanzarote.
2000–2500 BC	The islands are occupied by the Guanches, a tall, white race, thought to have been Berbers from north Africa; they speak a language recognisibly related to that of the Berbers.
82 BC	Roman sailors visit the two eastern Canary Islands. Greek and Roman tradition refers to the Canaries as the Fortunate Isles.
cAD 1	Juba II of Mauretania sends an expedition to explore the Fortunate Isles. All the islands are then named, one of them being called Canaria on account of its wild dogs (Latin *canis*, dog).
cAD 1000	Arab raiders pay a first visit, taking a few Guanche slaves; they call the islands Kaledat.
1312	Genoese sailor Lancelotto Malocello visits Fuerteventura and Lanzarote (which is a corruption of his name).
1339	Mallorcan cartographer Angelino Dolcet draws the first map showing the Canaries, though he only includes Fuerteventura and Lanzarote.
1341	A Genoese expedition reports that Fuerteventura (and perhaps Lanzarote) is covered in goats and trees.
1400–1500	French, English, Dutch and Arab pirates raid both islands, capturing both Guanche and mixed-blood slaves. Most are sold at Valencia, in Spain.
1402	Two Normans, Gadifer de la Salle and Jean de Béthencourt, land on Lanzarote, basing themselves on the Rubicón coastline (west of Playa Blanca). They claim the islands for the king of Spain.
1405	Béthencourt and de la Salle establish a first settlement on Fuerteventura at Betancuria and begin the process of colonisation.

1730–36	Timanfaya eruptions destroy a third of Lanzarote. Many islanders flee to Europe and South America.
1824	New volcanic eruptions add to the destruction and the layer of *malpaís*.
1919	César Manrique is born in Arrecife, Lanzarote. As a young man he leaves to study art, on the mainland, in Madrid.
1924	Don Miguel Unamuno is exiled to Fuerteventura, and praises its harsh simplicity.
1940s	Facist Spain is believed to use southern Fuerteventura to assist Nazis.
early 1960s	Package tourism to the Canaries begins.
1968	César Manrique returns to Lanzarote and completes his first major landscape work, Jameos del Agua. Timanfaya is named a protected natural area, and limitations are placed on its development.
1970	Timanfaya begins to receive tourists, and Manrique opens El Diablo restaurant.
1974	The Spanish Government declares Timanfaya a national park to be strictly protected.
1978	Manrique receives the World Ecology and Tourism Award.
1986	Manrique receives the Europa Nostra Award for conservation work on Lanzarote.
1990	Jardín de Cactus, the last of Manrique's tourist attractions, is completed.
1992	César Manrique is killed in a car accident at the Tahíche junction, on 25 September.
1993	Correlejo dunes on Fuerteventura are made a Natural Park. UNESCO declares the whole island of Lanzarote a world biosphere reserve.

Best of Lanzarote

Flames burst from a volcano vent whilst tourists stand their distance on the Islote de Hilario in the Parque Nacional de Timanfaya

A selection of local wines to accompany any meal, inside the Parque Nacional de Timanfaya restaurant at Islote de Hilario

If you only have a short time to visit Lanzarote and Fuerteventura, or would like to get a complete picture of the islands, here are the essentials:

- See twigs burst into flame on Islote de Hilario. The scorching ground temperature ignites brushwood and boils water in seconds (➤ 34).
- Take the bus tour from Islote de Hilario. It is the only way to get into the very heart of volcano country.
- Visit the Fundación César Manrique. The genius and flair of the man who made Lanzarote great can be felt in his former home (➤ 30), which is now an important art gallery.
- Go to the Jameos del Agua during the day just to gaze and wonder, or in the evening for a night out in an amazing setting (➤ 35).
- Eat *papas arrugadas con mojo*. These ultra-tasty, salty new potatoes are one of the best local specialities. *Mojo* is a traditional Canarian piquant sauce.
- Drink Lanzarote wine. If you think a barren volcanic landscape is not the best place to grow grapes, you haven't tried Lanzarote's cool, crisp and dry Malvasia white wines.
- Sunbathe on a golden beach, not the grainy black stuff more typical of the other Canaries. Lanzarote and Fuerteventura have long, wide stretches of fine pale sands.
- Walk ten paces on the *malpaís*. To understand just how unworkable this land is, try walking on it. The best place to try this is La Geria (➤ 47), where it's easy to pull over to the side of the road and get out of the car.
- Walk on giant sand dunes. On Lanzarote's Playa Blanca, or in Fuerteventura's Dunes Natural Park or Pared Isthmus, stroll on the rolling, drifting desert sandscapes.
- Take a trip to another island. Whether you're on Lanzarote or Fuerteventura, it's worth making a day trip to see the sights of the other. It's also fun to visit Isla Graciosa or Isla de Lobos.

LANZAROTE & FUERTEVENTURA
how to organise your time

A Walk Around Arrecife

The relaxed little capital of Lanzarote is where the real, modern life of the island is lived. Start at the tourist information office on the waterfront, an attractive pavilion made from volcanic stone and carved timbers.

INFORMATION

Distance 5km
Time 2 hours
Start/end point Tourist office
🍴 Ciao (➤ 62, £)
✉ 1 Calle La Esperanza
☎ 928 81 35 11

Walk north, with the sea on your right, along the promenade as far as the causeway. A narrow bridge leads onto the first of the causeways to the Castillo de San Gabriel (➤ 58), situated on Isolote de los Ingleses.

Return to the promenade and take the road ahead, Calle Leon y Castillo. Turn right into the short street Calle Ginés de Castro y Alverez. This comes to the church dedicated to San Ginés, Arrecife's patron saint (➤ 59).

Turn right and right again and follow the white-washed lanes to the Charco de San Ginés (➤ 58). Follow the quiet promenade that runs all the way round the Charco, including a bridge across the entrance to the lagoon. At the inland end of the lagoon short lanes lead back to Calle Leon y Castillo.

Turn left into Calle Leon y Castillo, towards the sea. Turn right at Calle Gen Goded and follow the direction of traffic along Calle Alferez Cabrera Tavio to Plaza de la Constitución. Cross the square to the far corner and turn left and right into Calle Luis Morote and follow this back street, with its glimpses of the sea.

The 16th-century Puente de las Bolas, with Castillo de San Gabriel in the background beyond the waters off Arrecife

On a busy corner dozens of café tables are set out beside Calle Dr Negrín. Stop here for a drink and maybe a bite to eat while you watch the world pass by. Ahead you can see the burnt-out Gran Hotel, Lanzarote's tallest (and ugliest) building.

Turn left along Avenida Mancomunidad. The road turns right and left to approach the promenade gardens and then to return to the tourist information pavilion.

A Drive In Northern Lanzarote

This trip around the northeastern half of the island explores a Lanzarote that is awesome, yet pretty. Avoid Sundays, as the Teguise market brings many people onto the route.

From Arrecife take the main road to Teguise. Note the Manrique mobile sculptures at the junction before Tahíche. César Manrique's extraordinary home is nearby (➤ 30).

Except for a strip of *malpaís* to the left of the road, most visible at Tahíche, the countryside is rolling hills of grass and, in spring, abundant wild flowers. As you approach Teguise, the hill of Guanapay, topped by Santa Bárbara Castle comes into view. Teguise (➤ 46) deserves a leisurely visit on foot.

Follow the road to Haría (➤ 51), which soon begins to climb and wind before descending to the town.

On the high plateaux and peaks there are windmills – not the picturesque and old-fashioned kind, but modern wind generators. The high, winding road is enjoyable to drive, with many outstanding views. In particular, the beautiful Mirador de Haría.

The descent into the green valley of Haría, dotted with palms, is delightful. Becoming straighter, the road continues to Yé. Turn left here to Mirador del Río (➤ 39) which deserves a stop. A narrow road to the left of the viewpoint is now closed to vehicles and makes a thrilling clifftop stroll.

Turn south again, at first on the same road; after 2km take a left fork and wind sharply downhill towards the coast. Jameos del Agua (➤ 35) and Cueva de los Verdes (➤ 28) are nearby.

Turn right onto the coast road, which skirts Arrieta, crosses the cactus fields and passes the Jardín de Cactus (➤ 37). At Tahíche, turn left to return to Arrecife.

INFORMATION

Distance 66km
Time 5 hours
Start/end point Arrecife
🍴 Restaurants (➤ 65) at Haría (££), and the Mirador del Rio (£)

Scattered whitewashed buildings form the village of Haría, seen from the Mirador del Haría

A Walk Exploring La Graciosa

Take the 10 o'clock ferry from Lanzarote to La Graciosa, which takes half an hour to reach La Graciosa's tiny port of Caleta del Sebo. The walk takes in Las Agujas (The Needles) and the Pedro Barba ridge, which form a mountain at the centre of the island.

Walk along the village quayside, then turn right (at the bar) on a footpath and then a dirt road towards the Pedro Barba ridge.

La Graciosa's two volcanoes stand either side of the track: Mojón to the left and Pedro Barba to the right. The third peak which comes into view between them is Montaña Clara, a separate island. Behind is a fine view of the village and Riscos de Famara.

At a fork keep right, and head towards the holiday homes at Pedro Barba. You are walking around the foot of Pedro Barba volcano. The rocky island of Alegranza comes into view.

Where the track forks again continue to the left. The right-hand path heads down to Pedro Barba village, which makes an agreeable diversion.

The track skirts the northern slopes of Pedro Barba, with dunes away to the right, and a sea view of Alegranza. Ahead rises Montaña Bermeja, and the cone of Pedro Barba comes into view again. As the track heads away from Pedro Barba and towards the foot of Montaña Bermeja, take a turn on the left which leads you back in the direction of Lanzarote. On the right is a spectacular beach of black rock and golden sand, called Playa de las Conchas. Ahead is the dramatic coast of Lanzarote.

A left turn takes the track south, again with Mojón on one side of the path (this time on the right) and Pedro Barba on the other. When the Riscos de Famara come into view, it's not much further to Caleta del Sebo.

INFORMATION

Distance 18km
Time 4 hours
Start point Caleta del Sebo
🚢 From Orzola at 10AM
🚌 Bus to Orzola leaves Arrecife at 7:40AM
End point Caleta del Sebo
🚢 Back to Orzola at 4PM
🚌 Bus to Arrecife leaves Orzola when ferry passengers have disembarked, at 4:30–5PM
🍴 Bars (£) Caleta del Sebo

A ferry prepares to leave from the harbour at Orzola on the north of the island for Caleta del Sebo, on the island of Graciosa

A Drive Around Timanfaya

This drive crosses the *malpaís*, or badlands, and includes the official coach tour, which offers the only way to see the most awesome region at the heart of the park. The Ruta de los Volcanes coach tour departs at roughly hourly intervals throughout the day from outside El Diablo restaurant on the summit of Islote de Hilario. The trip is included in the Islote entrance ticket.

From Yaiza drive due north on the Tinajo road. The dark, awesome *malpaís* of Timanfaya Plain (► 53) starts almost at once. After 3km, the Camel Park (► 52) appears beside the road on the left. A further 4km brings you to the ticket booth for Islote de Hilario (► 34). There can be long queues here. Park at the summit of Islote de Hilario. Having watched the wardens demonstrate the intense heat of the earth just below the surface, take the coach trip around the centre of the 18th-century volcanic eruptions.

Although geared to tourists, and with certain special effects on board – designed to conjure up the atmosphere and power of the volcanic activity – you're unlikely to be disappointed by this extraordinary and memorable drive.

The coach takes a winding narrow road to Montaña Rajada (► 52), one of the most impressive viewpoints, looking out across volcanic cones, collapsed underground tunnels and utter devastation reaching to the sea.

The landscape is not all dark – there are vivid colours in and around the volcanic cones. Below is the Valley of Tranquillity (► 53), which was buried in a downpour of volcanic particles.

The bus skirts Timanfaya itself, and several smaller volcanoes, before returning to Islote de Hilario. After walking and exploring in the small area permitted around the Islote, continue to Mancha Blanca, where the visitor centre is worth a look (► 38).

INFORMATION

Distance 30km, including
14km coach trip
Time About 2 hours.
Last coach trip at 5PM
Start point Yaiza
End point Mancha Blanca
🍴 Restaurante El Diablo(££)
✉ Islote de Hilario
☎ 928 84 00 57

The restaurant and administration centre on the Islote de Hilario serves only to accentuate this volcanic region's other-world appearance

17

A Walk Along The Tremesana Route

INFORMATION

Distance 3km
Time 2 hours
Start/end point Visitor centre
🍴 Take a picnic
❷ Need to book in advance

Unregulated walking is not permitted in Timanfaya National Park for fear of walkers injuring themselves on the uneven terrain, or damage being caused to the fragile lichens that live on the surface of the volcanic rock. It has taken over 200 years for even this minimal flora to get established.

There are two free guided walks supervised by the park authority. This, called the Tremesana Route, is the easier of the two. The visitor centre itself provides a fascinating introduction to this region (➤ 38).

The walk will start and end with a short minibus ride. From Yaiza, the group starts walking near the foot of Montaña Tremesana.

In this area, figs are cultivated, in stone half-circles to protect them from the wind (the trees, but not the ground they stand on, are private property). One particular stone half-circle is unique: look for it on the side of Tremesana, cleverly buttressed to stop it sliding down the mountain. Continue towards Caldera Rajada, ahead.

The rising sun catches the clouds over the volcanic landscape of Parque Nacional de Timanfaya, bathing them in a flame red glow

The volcano erupted from the side, splitting the mountain apart. The guide will point out amazing colours in the rocks, and explain how the eruption created hollow tubes just beneath the ground (which can be seen at close quarters at Jameos del Agua). Tell-tale signs, such as yellow sulphur stains, show the guide where these tunnels occur.

The route continues between two other volcanoes, Hernández and Encantada. The guide will describe the process of plant colonisation.

The walk finally arrives at a track near the foot of a volcano called Pedro Pericó. You will be picked up by minibus and returned to the visitor centre by way of Yaiza (➤ 48).

A Drive In Southern Lanzarote

This is a fascinating and enjoyable day out, taking in the island's extraordinary variety and some of its most exceptional sights.

From the Arrecife city ring road (Circunvalacíon) take the turn to San Bartolomé. Sray on this rural road until you reach the junction with the road to Uga and Yaiza, on the left. At this junction, close to the very centre of Lanzarote, is Manrique's strange cubist monument to the *campesino*, or peasant (➤ 40). Beside it is a small rural museum. Mozaga, straight ahead, has a good bodega (wine cellar), with shop.

Take the Uga and Yaiza road. Beware – it becomes narrow, with deep ditches on each side and passing is difficult in places. This road enters La Geria, where vines grow in hollows dug into bleak grey volcanic desert. After 13km it reaches the attractive village of Uga (➤ 51).

Turn right for Yaiza, just 3km away. The pretty village (➤ 48) lies on the edge of the dark *malpaís*. Stop for a walk and perhaps lunch.

Continue through Yaiza on the main Playa Blanca road. After some 3km, on the right beside a junction, are the strange geometric salt pans of Janubio. The road soon begins to cross the flat, rather bleak Rubicón plain. Follow it right into the resort of Playa Blanca (➤ 44). Spend an agreeable half-hour on the promenade of this small, modern beach resort. For a bigger beach, and fewer people, explore Papagayo (➤ 43).

Take the less-frequented, minor road 6km northeast towards Femés (➤ 51). Continue another 6km to the main road and turn right for Puerto del Carmen. The road winds steeply down into Puerto del Carmen (➤ 51), a lively, pleasant family resort, with a big beach backed by restaurants.

Take the main road past the airport back into Arrecife.

INFORMATION

Distance 70km
Time 5 hours
Start/end point Arrecife
🍴 La Era (££)
✉ Carretera General, Yaiza
☎ 928 83 00 16

The traditional low, white-painted houses of Yaiza

Finding Peace & Quiet

A TROPICAL WIND

Nearly all of Lanzarote and Fuerteventura's holiday accommodation is on south-facing coasts, which are sheltered from the prevailing trade winds (*alisios*, in Spanish). Trade winds, found only in tropical regions, blow from the northwest. Lying between the 28th and 29th parallels, Lanzarote and Fuerteventura are less than 645km from the Tropic of Cancer.

Cochineal beetles on an opuntia cactus

Lanzarote fennel gowing in Haría

It's hard not to get away from it all on Lanzarote, while on Fuerteventura it's even easier to escape the crowds. The tourist industry on both islands is confined to a small number of resorts, with huge areas of unspoiled countryside, dunes, beaches and volcanic *malpaís* all within a short distance.

EXPLORING

Use the road map from Lanzarote's tourist offices to find minor roads and tracks (some are in very poor condition) leading into the heart of deserted island scenery or down to empty beaches and bays. Or leave the crowd behind just by walking away along the long sandy beaches and rocky coasts.

Fuerteventura, too, is crossed by minor tracks and trails where neither tourists nor locals are much seen. With a four-wheel-drive, follow tracks on the Jandía Peninsula to beautiful, lonely sands. Beware, though, of swimming in such lonely places, especially on the west coast of Fuerteventura, as undercurrents can be dangerous.

NATURE RESERVES

Both islands have large protected zones where development has been forbidden, and where distinctive flora and fauna can be spotted. In fact, despite the seemingly barren landscape, Lanzarote and Fuerteventura are a haven for certain rare plants and birds and even harbour several native species unique to these two islands.

Lanzarote's offshore island, La Graciosa, though easily accessible by ferry from Orzola, is a place to find perfect solitude. The other, more remote islands, Montaña Clara and Alegranza, are breeding grounds for little shearwaters and Bulwer's petrels. In northern Lanzarote, the almost deserted sands of Famara beach are backed by rugged 700m tall cliffs, where Eleonora's falcons breed.

On and below the cliffs, yellow-flowering *Pulicaria canariensis fleabane*, *Argyranthemum ochroleucum*, looking like an unkempt ragwort, and the pretty yellow daisy bush *Astericus schultzii* flourish: all are unique to Lanzarote and Fuerteventura. On the clifftop grows *Ferula lancerottensis*, the umbellifer also unique to this location. You'll see, too, attractive Canarian varieties of the euphorbia succulents, which positively thrive around the islands' coasts, such as the swollen-stemmed *Euphorbia canariensis*.

Inland, the Famara heights descend into the lush Haría valley, where a gentle micro-climate creates a miniature world of flourishing palms, cacti and several unique species of plant.

DESERTSCAPES

Fuerteventura's dry, barren, unpopulated landscapes and the tracts of sand dunes are just the place to find peace and quiet, and discover the low, clinging plants that can live here. The sandy Jandía Peninsula gives its name to the red-flowered cactus-like *Euphorbia handiensis* succulent, found only on these beaches. Climb the high slopes behind to find the straggling blue-flowering *Echium handiense bugloss*, also unique to this island.

On both islands, the houbara bustard, cream-coloured courser and black-bellied sandgrouse – rare species elsewhere – are at home in the dry, desert-like *malpaís* and dunes. Several native birds seen here are paler versions of their European cousins, for example the rare Canarian chat, Berthelot's pipit and short-toed lark. You'll also see the trumpeter finch, with its short red beak, and hear its unmistakable call.

DID YOU KNOW?

Surprisingly, that well-known, bright yellow songbird called *Serinus canaria* is not seen here. The Canaries are not named after the birds, as some believe, but the other way round. The islands were called after quite a different native – wild dogs (the Latin *canis* means 'dog'), probably those found on Fuerteventura. A white-pawed local breed still survives, the descendant of the original inhabitants.

Between cracks and folds in rock that was once molten, small succulent plants have taken hold

The winds have drifted the sands, leaving undulating waves across the surface of the dunes at Corralejo

What's On

JANUARY
Cabalgata de los Reyes Magos Festival (Three Kings Parade, 5 Jan): Teguise.

FEBRUARY
Fiesta de Nuestra Señora de Candelaria (Candlemas, 2 Feb): a big festival and pilgrimage in Gran Tarajal and La Oliva, Fuerteventura.
Carnaval: especially exuberant in Arrecife on Lanzarote, and Corralejo on Fuerteventura.

MARCH/APRIL
Easter: look out for big events all over the islands during Easter Week.

JUNE
Fiesta de San Juan (24 Jun): celebrating the midsummer, Haría, Lanzarote.
Corpus Christi: Arrecife, Lanzarote. Patterns of coloured sand are used to decorate the ground.

JULY
Fiesta de Nuestra Señora de Regla (2 Jul): Pajara, Fuerteventura.
Fiesta de San Buenaventura (14 Jul): Betancuría, Fuerteventura, honours the town's patron saint and the island's incorporation into Spain.
Fiesta de Nuestra Señora del Carmen (16 Jul): Teguise, Lanzarote; Corralejo, Morro del Jable, Fuerteventura.
Fiesta (last Sat in Jul): La Pared, Fuerteventura.

AUGUST
Fiestas de Carmen (two weeks from 1 Aug): Puerto del Carmen, Lanzarote. On the last Saturday fishing boats put out to sea displaying charmingly decorated effigies of the saint.
Fiesta de San Ginés (whole month): everywhere, but especially Arrecife, Lanzarote. Processions, parades and traditional dancing in the streets.

SEPTEMBER
Fiesta de Nuestra Señora de Antigua (8 Sep): in honour of Antigua's patron saint, Fuerteventura.
Fiesta de Nuestra Señora de Guadalupe (8 Sep): Teguise, Lanzarote .
Virgen de los Volcanes (15 Sep): pilgrimage (*romería*) to Mancha Blanca, Lanzarote with re-enactment of the Virgin stopping the lava flow.
Fiesta de Nuestra Señora de la Peña (3rd Sat): Vega del Rio de Palma, Fuerteventura.
Fiesta (29 Sep): Tuineje, Fuerteventura.

OCTOBER
Fiesta de Nuestra Señora del Rosario (7 Oct): Puerto del Rosario, Fuerteventura. *Battle of Tamacita* (13 Oct): Tuineje, Fuerteventura.

NOVEMBER
Fiesta de San Diego de Alcalá (13 Nov): Gran Tarajal, Fuerteventura.

DECEMBER
Christmas: nativity plays and processions take place all over the islands.

LANZAROTE & FUERTEVENTURA's
top 25 sights

The sights are shown on the maps on the inside front cover and inside back cover, numbered **1**–**25** alphabetically

Arrecife

➕ D3

🍴 Cafés (£) on waterfront

❓ Annual Fiesta de San Ginés in August brings processions, parades and traditional dancing to the streets.

A bustling town with a population of 40,000, Arrecife still maintains its traditional and characterful seafaring roots.

Until the last century Arrecife was no more than a small working port. Inland Teguise was the island's capital and market centre, well away from the raiders who harried the coast. That is why Arrecife is still known to many locals simply as *el puerto*. To protect itself, Arrecife built the two fine fortresses, Castillo de San José and Castillo de San Gabriel, that still watch over its harbours today. As the coastal danger declined and trade increased, Arrecife grew, finally becoming the capital of Lanzarote in 1852.

If, while touring Lanzarote, you ever wonder 'Where is everybody?', the answer is simple, 'in Arrecife'. Today half the islanders live in the capital, and many more come here to work each day – the city is the islands administration and business centre. A striking, in some ways rather satisfying, contrast to the picturesque strangeness of the rest of the island, Arrecife is an ordinary, hardworking Spanish town making few concessions to tourists. Having expanded well before the days of César Manrique, this is the one place on the island that really does not conform to his aesthetic guidelines. Indeed, Lanzarote's most unsightly modern buildings are to be found here.

Hotels and other buildings beyond the fine golden sands of Playa Reducto

There are pretty places too. Sturdy little Castillo de San Gabriel, standing on the reef that gave the town its name (*arrecife* means reefs), gives charm to the busy waterfront main road. The town's excellent El Reducto main beach and its old harbour, with the waterside gardens and promenade, are a delight. The other places of interest, too, are all close to the sea, and the main tourist office is also here on Avenida Gen Franco.

Betancuría

Full of ancient charm, Betancuría nestles in the fertile lands of Fuerteventura's interior – waiting to be discovered.

Named after the 15th century Norman conqueror of this island, Jean de Béthencourt – Juan de Betancuría in Spanish – this bright white village in the very centre of Fuerteventura remained its capital until 1834. Betancuría still keeps something of its historic, aristocratic character. De Béthencourt built his capital here in the belief that being so far from the sea, it would be safe from the Moorish pirates who terrorised the coasts. He was proved wrong; pirates repeatedly sacked the town, in 1593 destroying the original Norman-style cathedral and taking away 600 captives as slaves.

The church was rebuilt in 1620, in an interesting hybrid style, with a painted ceiling, a fine baroque altarpiece and ancient gravestones forming part of the floor. It became a cathedral again in 1924. Many village houses still have façades and doorways dating from the 1500s and 1600s. Across the church square, a museum devoted to religious art displays de Béthencourt's original standard, the Pendón de la Conquista. A museum of archaeology, across the (usually dry) river, houses Guanche relics, which are exceptionally plentiful here.

INFORMATION

➕ IFC (Fuerteventura)

🍴 Simple bar-restaurant (£) beside Museo Arqueología

🚌 No 2 from Puerto del Rosario to Vega Rio Palma, twice daily

🔄 Ermitage de Nuestra Señora de la Peña (➤ 59), Antigua (➤ 50)

❓ The major local saint's day is San Buenaventura, 14 July

Museo Arqueológico

✉ 12–14 Calle Roberto Roldán

☎ 928 87 82 41

🕐 Tue–Sat 10–5, Sun 10–2. Closed Mon

💰 Inexpensive

The high altar in Betancuría's 'cathedral' of 1620; replacing the earlier Cathedral of Santa Maria, destoyed in 1539

Corralejo

INFORMATION

- IFC (Fuerteventura)
- 30km north of Puerto del Rosario
- Wide choice of restaurants (£–££)
- No 6 via Puerto del Rosario, hourly; No 7 runs via La Oliva
- To Isla de Lobos (☎ 928 86 62 38) To Playa Blanca (☎ 928 53 50 90)
- Plaza Pública (☎ 928 86 62 35)
- Isla de Lobos (➤ 33), La Oliva (➤ 42)

Fishing in Corralejo Harbour

Backed by the most impressive section of the Fuerteventura Dunes, Corralejo is a wonderful, and popular, centre for a beach holiday.

Though still a working fishing harbour and a pleasant small town, this is Fuerteventura's biggest and most accessible beach resort. Lying on the breezy northern tip of the island, just across the narrow strait from tourist developments on the southern tip of Lanzarote, Corralejo has woken up to the fact that it too has that magic formula 'sun, sea and sand'. As a consequence, several hotels and apartment complexes have opened. For sun, its record can hardly be matched anywhere else in the Canaries. When it comes to sand, although the sandy white beach in town is not very large, immense golden beaches and mountainous dunes stretch out just behind the town and go on for miles (➤ 29). The heart of the town centres on a bustling square with shops, bars and budget restaurants, and there is a more bustling nightlife than in other resorts on Fuerteventura.

Castillo de San José

An important collection of modern art is housed in this beautiful little semi-circular stone fortress on a clifftop overlooking the sea.

The commanding position of San José Castle once made it a vital defence for the island's capital and port against the pirates who plagued the Canaries. Today it looks down on the busy commercial harbour of Puerto de Naos.

Built of black basalt in the midst of a period of great suffering after the eruption of Timanfaya, the castle came to be known as the Hunger Fortress. It is entered by crossing a moat, and the year of its completion, 1779, is carved above the entrance. Despite its strictly military purpose, the two-storey castle possesses great elegance and charm both inside and out. Its spacious halls and spiral stairwells, and the sharp contrast of black stone and white walls, create an atmosphere of powerful, stark simplicity. Floors are paved with patterned black volcanic slabs and black pebbles. The barrel-vaulted ceilings, too, are black.

In 1976 César Manrique restored the castle and installed the Museo Internacional de Arte Contemporáneo (International Museum of Contemporary Art) devoted to abstract modern art. The fantastic juxtaposition of vivid 20th-century forms and the black 18th-century fortress is startling, especially just inside the dark entrance, where a modern sculpture in glistening white marble stands. However, the paintings are poorly labelled and no catalogue is available.

Spiral steps lead down to César Manrique's own contribution, a glass-walled restaurant and bar overlooking the sea, with black tables, black napkins and modern classical music playing.

INFORMATION

+ D3
* Puerto Naos, 3km north of Arrecife on Costa Teguise road
* 928 81 23 21
* Museum 11–9, Castle 11–1
* Restaurant (£££), bar (£)
* Every 30 minutes from Arrecife waterfront, every hour at weekends and festivals
* Avenida Gen Franco, Arrecife (928 81 37 92)
* Few
* Free
* Castillo de San Gabriel (➤ 58)

Cueva de los Verdes

INFORMATION

➕ E2

✉ Near Arrieta (26km north of Arrecife)

☎ 928 17 32 20

🕐 Daily 10–6 (last tour at 5)

🍴 Casa Miguel (£), Arrieta waterfront (► 62)

🚌 No 9 about 1km away

ℹ Avenida Gen Franco, Arrecife (☎ 928 81 37 92)

♿ None (unsuitable for anyone who cannot walk and bend with ease)

💷 Moderate

↔ Los Jameos del Agua (► 35)

The guided 2km walk through part of one of the longest lava cave systems in the world is enhanced by lighting, music and natural illusions.

Monte Corona is an extinct volcano in northern Lanzarote, whose eruptions some 5,000 years ago created a *malpaís* – a contorted, blackened landscape similar to Timanfaya at the other end of the island. The Corona eruptions formed one of the world's longest lava caves, Cueva de los Verdes and neighbouring Jameos del Agua being part of the same 7.5km Corona system (of which 1.5km is beneath the seabed). These hollow tubes were carved out as older basalt rock was melted and washed away by the lava flowing around it, and underground gases inflated the molten terrain.

The network of caverns and tunnels has long been known to locals, who used to hide here during the 17th century when Arab slave hunters and pirates raided the island. Cueva de los Verdes (not in fact a 'green' cave – Verde was the family name of former owners) is a short section reached by descending to a tunnel below ground level. Hour-long guided visits in English take visitors along a circular 2km walkway, narrow and low-ceilinged in places. Haunting music and lighting heighten the experience, which takes in vividly coloured rocks, a large hall called the Refuge, which can only be entered by one person at a time, impressive rock formations and a clever optical illusion at the end of the tour.

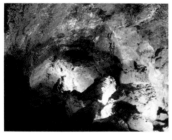

Deep purples and green highlight the roof of a section of the atmospherically lit tunnels of the Cueva de los Verdes

The entrance and ticket booth to the caves have been discreetly arranged to avoid disfiguring the barren seashore *malpaís*, which can be explored on footpaths.

The Dunes of Fuerteventura

The sun-dried, windswept island has immense beaches and tranquil, empty regions of fabulous sand dunes stretching as far as the eye can see.

Like a miniature Sahara, the island of Fuerteventura is sandy and waterless, windy and parched. For millennia sands have blown here across the 60 miles from Africa, covering the volcanic layer beneath, creating endless dune landscapes and great hills of pale sand.

Right behind Fuerteventura's main resort, Corralejo, on the island's northern tip, rises its largest and most impressive single area of dunes. This complex system of dazzling pale sands, stretching about 10km along the coast and reaching 2–3km inland from the shore, has been declared a protected zone known as the Parque Natural de las Dunas de Corralejo. Despite this conservation status, two popular package-holiday hotels stand within the park's limits, the Tres Islas and Oliva Beach. They pre-date the creation of the park.

Fuerteventura has another major dune area at the Isthmo de la Pared, the narrow isthmus of mountainous dunes separating Jandía Peninsula from the rest of the island. At some stage in prehistory, the dunes did not exist and Jandía was a separate volcanic island.

Fuerteventura's dunes are neither barren nor lifeless. As well as forming spectacular beaches, they also support unusual plant species that can thrive in these dry, salty sands. Some are found only here, including a yellow-flowering shrub, *Lotus lancerottense*, *Echium handiense* with its bluebell flowers, and a red-flowered succulent, *Euphorbia handiensis*.

INFORMATION

🔗 IFC (Fuerteventura)

🍴 Hotels Tres Islas has restaurants (£-££) and bars. Restaurants (£) in Corralejo. Also La Pared (£) and Costa Calma (£-££) at La Pared

🚌 No 6 (Corralejo–Puerto del Rosario)

🚢 To Corralejo from Playa Blanca on Lanzarote takes 40 minutes

✈ Airport just south of the Parque Natural

🛈 Plaza Grande, Corralejo (☎ 928 86 62 35); the shopping centre, Morro Jable (☎ 928 54 07 76)

🔄 Corralejo (► 26), Isla de Lobos (► 33), La Oliva (► 42), Jandía Peninsula (► 36)

The dunes at Corralejo

29

Fundación César Manrique

INFORMATION

➕ D3

✉ Taro de Tahíche, 5km
north of Arrecife

☎ 928 84 31 38 or 928 84
30 70

🕐 Mon–Sat 10–6

🍴 Snack bar (£)

🚌 No 7 (Arrecife–Teguise),
No 9 (Arrecife–Orzola),
several times daily each
way, stop at Tahíche

ℹ 6 Avenida Gen Franco,
Arrecife (☎ 928 81 37
92)

♿ Few

💷 Moderate

↔ Arrecife (➤ 24)

*Plantlife in the grounds
of the Fundación César
Manrique, a museum
dedicated to the life and
work of the artist*

**César Manrique's own home, half
submerged in a string of volcanic bubbles in the rock, displays to the full his
tremendous artistic flair.**

Manrique had a special interest in mobiles and
one extraordinary example is the huge complex
of colour and movement – like an enormous
children's toy – standing at the entrance to his
own home. It is best seen at night, when the
mobile and the house are not so much illumi-
nated as dotted with light.

Here architecture is fun, astonishing and brilliant. The visible exterior of the building,
inspired by traditional local style, combines
dazzling white with jet black. Around it, a
garden of cacti, succulents and semicircles of
stone is set between white and black walls.
Immense cylindrical cacti look like green Doric
columns. Above the doorway, note Manrique's
'logo' – an interlocked C and M said to resemble
a devil.

Since Manrique's death, the interior has
become an art gallery, consisting mainly of
his private collection. It includes works by
most of the big names of 20th-century
abstract and modern art, including Tapies,
Míro and Picasso, as well as a number of
Manrique's own powerful canvases.

Steps lead down into five volcanic
bubbles (created during the eruptions of
1730–36), each made into a complete
room with distinctive character, colour
and furniture. One has a trickling foun-
tain, another a palm tree growing up
through the roof. The dining room has an
open grill, a pool filled from a black water-
spout, and a dining table beneath a ceiling of rock. Narrow galleries in the rock,
painted white and black to match the rest
of the house, link the bubble rooms.

El Golfo

A spectacular fusion of colours, El Golfo was once a harbour, but volcanic eruptions created the bar that now divides the lagoon from the sea.

On the southwestern shore of the island, El Golfo is the extraordinary result of a meeting between the blackened volcanic devastation of Timanfaya and the power of the Atlantic waves. Here the half-submerged cone of a volcano has been eroded and transformed into a bizarre natural attraction. Over time, the ocean has eaten into the volcanic crater, leaving a lagoon surrounded by an amphitheatre of lava cliff, the rock streaked and stained with a multitude of strange reds and russets.

Most remarkable is the colour of the lagoon. A number of factors, including volcanic minerals and algae, have given the water a deep, intense emerald hue, especially brilliant when it catches the sun, and a very striking contrast to the glorious blue sea that lies beside it. Although linked to the ocean, the lagoon appears quite separate from it – the connection is through volcanic passages hidden underground.

To reach the lagoon, follow the access road on the left 2km before the village of El Golfo. On reaching the car park continue on foot, following signs for a short walk around the headland.

Between El Golfo village and the lagoon there are a number of sheltered bays with black beaches. The seashore village of El Golfo itself has rather an end-of-the-road feel, but has become a centre for enticing fish restaurants.

INFORMATION

* B3
* 12km northwest of Yaiza
* About a dozen small restaurants (£) in El Golfo village serve fresh fish and shellfish
* Free
* Los Hervideros (► 59), Timanfaya (► 52), Yaiza (► 48)

Beneath steep cliffs of black, yellow and grey, a lagoon, usually emerald green (coloured by the algal growth in the water), lies in the rim of half a volcanic crater, the other half of which is submerged in the sea at El Golfo

La Graciosa

An impressive overview of Graciosa Island and the harbour fronts buildings confined to the one area; as seen from Mirador Del Río

Named *Grace* by the sailors who discovered the island, Lanzarote's offshore jewel is a treasure for those seeking tranqillity and solitude.

La Graciosa is the island that rests at the centre of the view from the Mirador del Río (➤ 39). For many who come to admire it, this is as near as they get to the island. However, La Graciosa is easily reached and a trip there makes an enjoyable day out.

Administratively, La Graciosa is part of Lanzarote. The channel (El Río) between the two islands is just 2km wide, though the ferry goes the long way round and takes 30–45 minutes. With a total area of only 41sq km, the island is small enough for keen walkers to circumnavigate in a day; it receives few visitors and is a haven of tranquillity.

Yet La Graciosa is not quite as deserted as might be thought. It has two sleepy fishing villages, Caleta del Sebo (literally 'Greasy Cove', named after the whale blubber found on the beach) and Pedro Barba, both on the channel between the two islands, as well as superb golden sandy beaches and a couple of simple bar-restaurants and basic *pensiones*. And the view from La Graciosa towards the Riscos de Famara and Mirador del Río is almost as good as the view from Lanzarote. Perhaps the island's most enjoyable feature is the lack of cars – no motor vehicles are allowed. There aren't even any roads.

Away from the shore, La Graciosa consists of dunes and treeless volcanic terrain. Despite this, it was at La Graciosa that Norman conqueror Jean de Béthencourt first stepped ashore after his journey from Europe.

Isla de Lobos

This curious island has no restaurants and no shade, yet makes an enjoyable day out. Take a picnic, and be prepared for the breeze and glaring sunshine.

Lying some 3km offshore from Corralejo, the tiny Island of the Seals – as its name literally translates – is a haunting miniature world, a curious landscape of tiny volcanic protrusions rising from stones and sand. Was it so named for real seals, as some claim? There are no seals here now. Perhaps instead the *lobos* were the little rock mounds, which do look from afar like animals lying on a beach. The once-volcanic Montaña Lobos, just 127m high, rises above the rest. Despite being a popular boat outing for tourists, the island has no roads, no vehicles and no inhabitants, and so remains an unspoiled haven of calm and simplicity.

It takes less than an hour to reach the *faro* (lighthouse) at Punta Martiño, at the opposite end of the island to the ferry drop-off. From here there is a great view back across Lobos and Fuerteventura and, the otherway, to the pale beaches on Lanzarote's southern shore.

INFORMATION

- ✛ IFC (Fuerteventura)
- ✉ 3km off shore from Corralejo
- 🍴 Small café/kiosk (£) at quayside. Order lunch on arrival or take a picnic and plenty of water with you
- 🚢 Small ferry from Corralejo at 10AM, return boat at 4PM
- ↔ Corralejo (► 26)

The glass-bottomed boat which ferries pasengers to and from the Islote del Lobos; the glass bottom enables passengers to enjoy the clear unspoiled waters

Islote de Hilario

INFORMATION

➕ B3

✉ Timanfaya National Park,
7km north of Yaiza

☎ 928 84 00 57

🕐 Summer, daily 10–6,
winter, daily 10–5

🍴 El Diablo (££) restaurant
and snack bar

🚌 None, but many coach
excursions from resorts

ℹ Avenida de las Playas,
Puerto del Carmen
☎ 928 51 53 37

♿ Few

💷 Moderate (includes
Volcano Route bus tour)

🔁 Timanfaya National Park
(► 52), Yaiza (► 48),
Ermita de los Dolores
(► 59)

❓ The last Volcano Route
tour leaves at 4pm. For
car drivers, there are
extensive free parking
facilities

Water bursts forth from a geyser whilst tourists keep their distance

The heart and soul of Lanzarote is an awesome red and black volcano called Islote de Hilario or Fire Mountain, whose presence dominates the island.

Lanzarote's Fire Mountain is still alive but taking a nap. Every visitor to the island is drawn to its summit. Visible from afar, the volcano dominates the view and the thoughts of visitors and locals alike. Its catastrophic force once destroyed in an instant the livelihood of most of the islanders, yet it is now Lanzarote's most stunning attraction. Black and red, fiery and ferocious, the swirling, sculpted terrain all around leaves no doubt that this is truly a volcano with a temper. Here and there tortured rocks are streaked with colour, where stones have melted and fused in the heat. The spectacular *malpaís* – badlands – all around the mountain show not a blade of grass, but do support lichen and small plants.

The usual way to climb the volcano is to drive along a roadway that climbs to the summit of Islote de Hilario, where the lingering volcanic heat remains hottest. At the very top, a big, crowded and convivial restaurant called El Diablo (The Devil) is an incongruous oasis of life and enjoyment amid the tortured, arid wilderness. Conceived and constructed by César Manrique, the restaurant is a glass-walled circle giving huge, thrilling views of the volcanic terrain and the sea beyond. Before you go into El Diablo, take a look at the wide opening resembling a well, just by the entrance. This 'well' descends into fiery earth, not water, and the restaurant's meat and fish are cooked in the oven-like 300°C heat that wafts up from the volcano. At other places close by, the surface of the ground is too hot to walk on, sometimes reaching 100°C. Ten centimetres below, the temperature is 140°C; at 6m down it is 400°C; while the temperature just 13m underground reaches 600°C.

Jameos del Agua

César Manrique turned this bizarre volcanic feature into one of the island's most intriguing sights, an exotic subterranean water garden

A *jameos* is an underground volcanic tunnel whose roof has partly collapsed. Until Manrique set to work, this one was just a hole in the ground.

Jameos del Agua is reached from the surface by spiral wooden stairs that twist down into the earth. At the bottom, astonishingly, a restaurant and dance floor look over an eerie underground lake; tiny, blind white crabs live in its perfectly transparent water. At the lake's far end, the arty tables of another bar perch on little terraces where you can sit with a meal or a drink.

This mysterious environment, within a roof-less cavern below sea level, is truly hard to comprehend at first. Whatever the weather outside, here the air is still and balmy, and full of the songs of tiny birds.

From the bar, meandering paths lead upwards among rocks and plant beds to a dazzling man-made blue and white pool. Behind it, a large cave accommodates a 500-seat auditorium used for shows, concerts and meetings! More spiral steps wind steeply up to the edges of the *jameos*, giving thrilling views down into this extraordinary meeting point of man and nature.

At the top, the Casa de los Volcanes (House of Volcanoes) is a science museum that is devoted, unsurprisingly, mainly to volcanic activity.

After dark on Tuesday, Friday and Saturday, Jameos del Agua becomes a popular nightclub where crowds drink, dine and dance in the spectacular surroundings.

INFORMATION

+ E2
- Near Arrieta, 26km north of Arrecife
- 928 84 80 20
- Daily 9:30–6:45; also Tue, Fri, Sat 7PM–3AM (folklore show at 11PM)
- Restaurant (££, evenings only), two bars (£, all day)
- No 9 (Arrecife–Orzola)
- None
- Moderate
- Cuevos de los Verdes (► 28)
- Concerts and lectures held in the auditorium, and seminars in the Casa de los Volcanes. Details from tourist offices

A concert hall - designed by Manrique - cut into the volcanic rock

Jandía Peninsula

INFORMATION

- ✚ IFC (Fuerteventura)
- ✉ 80km south of Puerto del Rosario
- 🍴 At Morro del Jable, numerous eateries (£–££) on the beachside promenade
- 🚌 No 1 from Puerto del Rosario to Morro del Jable via all the resorts and beach stops of the eastern Jandía (six times daily). Bus 4 and 9, once daily each way, from Morro del Jable to inland Pájara (No 4 goes via Gran Tarajal, No 9 via La Pared), stopping at all the resorts. No 5 runs up and down the coast between Costa Calma and Morro del Jable about every hour from 9:30–9:30
- 🚢 A regular jetfoil service connects Morro del Jable with the islands of Gran Canaria and Tenerife
- ❓ Local fiestas on the Jandía Peninsula include 16 Jul at Morro del Jable and the last Sat in Jul at La Pared

In the south, Fuerteventura narrows at the sandy Pared Isthmus, before widening again to form the Jandía Peninsula, originally a separate island.

An awesome land of vast skies and vast beaches, the peninsula is overlooked by Fuerteventura's loftiest peak, the 807m-high extinct Pico de Zarza volcano (also known – you'll understand why as soon as you see it – as Orejas de Asno, 'donkey ears'). All around the steep upland there are long wide swathes of pale sand and immense unspoiled beaches.

On the peninsula's eastern shore, Playa de Sotavento de Jandía, or simply Sotavento, has 28km of sand. It's the site of the annual World Windsurfing Championships, though what makes this a windsurfer's heaven is being protected from the worst of the prevailing winds (Sotavento means 'leeward'). The unappealing Costa Calma development lies at one end of the beach.

South of Sotavento, the coast turns sharply west to the unsightly developments around Jandía Playa resort and to Morro del Jable, the peninsula's main town, which has a pleasant promenade, bars and eating places, and a fishing harbour. Beyond, the extreme tip of the island is edged with lovely, secretive sandy bays.

On the western side, the broad golden sandy sweep of Playa de Cofete and Playa de Barlovento ('windward') are beautiful but windy, with powerful undercurrents that are dangerous for swimmers. Inland, close to the shacks of Cofete, is the isolated mansion of Herr Gustav Winter, the enigmatic German owner of the whole Jandía Peninsula during and after World War II. Stories abound about Winter (who was given the land by General Franco) and his guests and his relations with the German, Spanish and Latin American regimes.

Jardín de Cactus

Transformed by César Manrique this disused quarry is now an extraordinary formal garden with over 1,400 varieties of cactus.

The fields of cactus around Guatiza and Mala, north of Arrecife, used to be cultivated as homes to a cochineal beetle, whose larva provides a bright red dye. Now the most striking landmark in the cactus district is César Manrique's towering 8m green metal cactus outside the entrance to his Cactus Garden.

Formerly a hand-dug quarry from which local farmers extracted volcanic rock, the garden is an oval-shaped enclosure descending in narrow concentric stone terraces. Each terrace is now covered with *picón*. Growing from the black ash like bizarre artworks are 1,420 species of cactus, a total of almost 10,000 plants, each standing separate from the rest and demanding attention.

Some are like porcupines, some like wedding cakes covered in hair, some like prickly rockets, some spreading themselves like octopuses, others uncoiling like snakes. Some resemble rolls of barbed wire. Others seem to have come straight out of a Wild West cartoon strip. Many have florid, gaudy blooms, others tiny, delicate flowers, sometimes strung around the plant like a necklace.

Visitors walk carefully around the terraces, gradually descending to a lower central area, where there is a miniature water garden and remnants of the quarry. A terrace rather wider than the rest accommodates a stylish bar, where circular wooden tables under pale sailcloth awnings offer a view of the entire garden.

Behind the bar, an old windmill rises above the garden and the surrounding landscape. Beautifully restored, it is still used for grinding grain.

INFORMATION

➕ E2
✉️ Guatiza (17km northeast of Arrecife)
📞 928 52 93 97
🕐 Daily 10–5:45
🍴 Bars/restaurant (£) 10–5PM
🚌 No 7 (Arrecife–Teguise)
ℹ️ Avenida Gen Franco, Arrecife (📞 928 81 37 92)
♿ Few
💰 Inexpensive
🔄 Teguise (➤ 46)

The Jardín de Cactus in Guatiza. The dry climate allows these plants to thrive and the gardens are home to over 10,000 species; the finger-shaped volcanic rocks are a regular feature of the gardens

Mancha Blanca Centro de Interpretación

INFORMATION

➕ C3

✉ 9km from Isolote de
Hilario, at Mancha Blanca

🕐 Daily 9–5

🍴 El Diablo restaurant (££)
on the Islote de Hilario
summit

🚌 None

♿ Few

💲 Free

↔ Islote de Hilario (➤ 34),
Ermita de los Dolores
(➤ 59)

The creation of the Canary Islands by volcanic means is charted here through a wealth of displays, diagrams and models.

Located on the park boundary, near the village of Mancha Blanca, the visitor centre must count as one of the park's most interesting sights – and one of the few man-made items in the landscape. The building at first appears small and low, its whiteness a sharp contrast with the dark lava. However, it turns out to be much larger, much of the centre lying underground. Inside is a cool, calm environment of white and black surfaces and polished wood, with exhibitions about the park, a library, bookshop, and administration areas, as well as viewpoints onto the volcanic terrain. Among the most interesting exhibits is the Eruption Hall, simulating the ground movements at the time of the 1730 volcanic eruption here. Note that no guides, no smoking and no noise are allowed at the centre.

Mirador del Río

A touch of Manrique magic has made a clifftop view of little Isla Graciosa into one of the loveliest places on the island.

A mirador is a viewpoint, and El Río, literally 'the river', is the name of the narrow strait between Lanzarote and its little sister island, Isla Graciosa. Outside the Mirador, one of Manrique's open metalwork signs stands in front of a daunting stone wall that actually conceals the view, with just a porthole hinting at what lies on the other side.

Before César Manrique set to work an old artillery post, Batería del Río, perched here, 479m high on the Famara cliffs with a commanding view over La Graciosa and the islands of Montaña Clara and Alegranza beyond.

Manrique's first thought was to create a restaurant here. He had a large room chipped out of the cliff top, and roofed it with two domes covered with earth and grass. It is entered through a long, winding white tunnel and spiral staircase, which plays with brilliant effect on the themes of light, space and air.

The white room – or rooms, for the domes break up the space – is exquisite, its simplicity, clarity and spaciousness a delight to the eye. Neat wooden tables provide a place to sit and relax, and a most unusual-looking bar serves drinks and snacks. There is also a balcony, where you can stand in the open air by a sheer drop.

The main attraction, however, is the view itself, a spectacular vista of sea and sky, in which La Graciosa floats as if itself suspended like a sculpture.

INFORMATION

- 🕂 E1
- ✉ 7km north of Haría
- ☎ 928 17 35 38
- 🍴 Snack bar (£)
- 🚻 None
- 🚌 To visit La Graciosa, catch a ferry from nearby Orzola
- ℹ Avenida Gen Franco, Arrecife (☎ 928 81 37 92)
- ♿ None
- 🎟 Inexpensive
- ↔ Haría (➤ 51)

A curious wrought iron sculpture by the artist César Manrique, designed as a sign on entering Mirador del Río

Monumento al Campesino

A traditional water purifier on display in the Monumento al Campesino

Situated at the heart of the island, Manrique's monument to the farming community of Lanzarote is said to depict a farmer, his cat and a rat.

The *campesino* is the countryman, the peasant farmer and man of the soil, whom César Manrique considered to be the very backbone of every nation, and the foundation on which its history and culture stands.

The white Campesino Monument is Manrique's tribute to the hard-working farming people of Lanzarote, who have long battled with the inhospitable terrain of their native island. Deeply moved by the labours that created the vineyards of La Geria (► 47), he named the 15m-high work El Monumento Fecundidad al Campesino Lanzaroteño (The Fertility Monument to the Lanzarote Peasant). Manrique dedicated the sculpture, which stands

prominently at a road junction outside the wine village of Mozaga, 'to the forgotten endeavours of the unknown farmers of Lanzarote'.

The enigmatic cubist monument was constructed in 1968 from farm debris, water tanks and old fishing boats.

The Casa Museo del Campesino is a copy of a fine traditional farm building and farmyard presented as a pristine black, white and green artwork. You can see an old preserved kitchen, tools and equipment, as well as a reproduction of a cottage workshop. In keeping with Manrique's ideas, an attractive farm-style restaurant at the site serves Lanzarote dishes.

Museo Agricola el Patio

A wonderful open-air establishment with restored windmill, this museum attempts to inject a shot of traditional farming life into today's modern world.

In a suitably rural location at the centre of the island, this museum of rural life gives an opportunity to see and learn about Lanzarote's intriguing, ingenious and unusual agricultural traditions. More than a museum, this is a peaceful, immaculately restored traditional farm, where visitors are guided round to take a close look inside one of the restored windmills and farm buildings, see a garden of cacti and other island plants, and contemplate the displays of farm tools, local architecture, ancient ceramics, and photographs of Lanzarote's traditional hard-working rustic lifestyle. To round off the tour, at the end of the visit you may taste wines actually produced on the estate.

INFORMATION

* C3
* Just outside Tiagua on the road to Sóo
* 928 52 91 06
* Mon–Fri 10–5:30, Sat 10–2:30. Closed Sun
* Simple, pleasant bar (£) on site
* No 13 (Arrecife–Sóo)
* Few
* Moderate
* The Campesino Monument and Museum (► 40)

El Patio's perfectly restored windmill. Inside, all the components have been crafted traditionally

La Oliva

INFORMATION

- 🏥 IFC (Fuerteventura)
- ✉ 17km south of Corralejo
- 🍴 Cafés in village (£)
- 🚌 No 7 (Puerto del Rosario to Corralejo) stops here twice daily each way
- 🔄 Monumento a Don Miguel de Unamuno (➤ 59), Corralejo (➤ 26)
- ❓ Our Lady of Candelaria is the big fiesta on 2 Feb

Centro de Arte Canario
- ☎ 928 86 82 33
- 🕐 Mon–Sat 10–6 (10–5 in winter). Closed Sun
- 💷 Moderate

Casa de la Cilla, Museo del Grano
- ☎ 928 85 14 00
- 🕐 Tue–Fri, Sun 9:30–5:30
- 💷 Inexpensive

This agreeable village brings together the island of Fuerteventura's history and its variety of imposing terrain in one hit.

Built in the early 17th century as a residence for Fuerteventura's military governors, this little town was the island's seat of government until 1880. Several fine old mansions, once homes of officials and wealthy landowners, survive from those days, though some are now derelict. The grandest of them is the long white La Casa de los Coroneles (the Colonels' House) or La Casa de la Marquesa, dating from 1650 and once belonging to the Cabrera Béthencourt family – their family crest can be seen above the entrance. Near by, the surprising and enjoyable Centro de Arte Canario showcases modern art from the islands. A new attraction is the Casa de la Cilla, Museo del Grano, an old granary with a small exhibition.

On the road to Villaverde, windmills are a reminder that this area was a centre for production of *gofio*. North of the town rises sandy 420m-high Montaña Arena.

A crumbling florid wooden balcony is attached to the side of the cream coloured Casa de los Coroneles in La Oliva, which now a romantic ruin, was once the grand home of the military commander of the island

Papagayo

Strictly for beach connoisseurs and determined sun-seekers, this stretch of golden sands remains fairly unspoiled – for the moment.

Breezy Punta de Papagayo (Papagayo Point) and the more sheltered sandy bays either side of it lie at Lanzarote's southernmost tip. These are just about the finest beaches on the island: sweeps of fine golden sand edged by the clear waters of the channel separating Lanzarote from Fuerteventura. Oddly, these excellent beaches can prove hard to find, and some still have to be reached on unmade roads with few, if any, signposts to guide the driver. Despite this, they do attract plenty of visitors, and they can get almost crowded at times.

The main beach, Playa de Papagayo (*papagayo* means parrot), is barely more than 15 minutes' drive from the resort town of Playa Blanca. Thanks to a newly completed road straight from Playa Blanca (just continue a little way past Águila), this is the most popular beach.

The ruined hamlet of El Papagayo, which is also signposted, is now home to sun-loving hippies. A string of other lovely beaches stretching around the peninsula of Punta de Papagayo, backed by sandy cliffs, are best reached on foot: Playa de los Pozos, Playa de Mujeres, and beyond the point, the nudists' secluded favourite, Playa de Puerto Muelas or La Caleta del Congrio. Be warned, however: none of these beaches has any shade, so you will have to carry your own.

All along this sandy stretch of coast, there are superb views to Fuerteventura – and from high points on the cliffs you can even see Puerto del Carmen and Arrecife. It seems certain that as time passes this part of Lanzarote will become a major tourist centre.

INFORMATION

➕ B4

✉ 6km east of Playa Blanca on the coast road

🍴 Bar–restaurant (£) at Playa Papagayo

🚌 Nearest bus service is at Playa Blanca

♿ None

🔄 Playa Blanca (➤ 44)

A small group sunbathing on the sand at Playa Blanca at Papagayo, in the area of Costa Rica's planned, controversial beach development which covers 2,000 hectares of an idyllic peninsula of sheltered coves

Playa Blanca

INFORMATION

➕ B4

✉ 35km from Arrecife

🍴 Bars and snack bars (£)
and restaurants (£–££) on
the promenade.
Restaurante Brisa Marina
(££) serves fresh fish,
seafood and Canarian
specialties

🚌 No 6 from Arrecife or
Puerto del Carmen to
Playa Blanca. There are
about 6 departures daily,
and the journey takes
around an hour

🚢 To Corralejo, on
Fuerteventura, several
times daily. There are
also ferries to Lobos
Island, in between the
two larger islands

♿ Few

🔁 Timanfaya National Park
(➤ 52), El Golfo (➤ 31)

This purpose-built resort on the island's southern shore basks in a sheltered position where both the wind and the waves are subdued.

The town's pleasant, golden sandy main beach catches the sun, is perfectly protected from the breeze, and is backed (in town) by an attractive promenade with plenty of greenery and café tables. There are two smaller beaches east of the centre, and another attractive beach area, with a sheltered little bay of fine sand and gentle waters, west of the port.

For the moment, Playa Blanca remains a quiet little place, with an away-from-it-all feeling that belies the fact that it is only 15km on a fast road across the Rubicón plain to Yaiza, and is therefore very conveniently placed for visiting Timanfaya National Park and all the sights of the southern half of the island.

From Playa Blanca's seashore you can look across the 11km channel between Lanzarote and Fuerteventura for a clear view of Fuerteventura and, in front of it, the small dark volcanic shape of Isla de Lobos. Ferries cross to Fuerteventura several times a day from Playa Blanca's main harbour for an easy and enjoyable day excursion. Fishing boats use the harbour too, and restaurants along the promenade feature plenty of freshly caught fish. There's also a bustling pleasure harbour.

Playa Blanca is the farthest south of Lanzarote's resorts, a relatively long way from the sights in the north, but it has some clear advantages for those who want sun, sea and sand, good food and a peaceful atmosphere. With almost nothing here before the resort was built, it is dedicated to holiday enjoyment. Most entertainment is provided by the hotels, which in Playa Blanca are of a high standard and most just a few paces from the sea.

Playa Grande

A 2–kilometre expanse of beautiful sand littered with watersports facilities, sun-shades and deckchairs provides the perfect holiday beach.

The town's main beach, a delightful wide band of yellow sand, runs alongside busy Avenida de las Playas, main artery of the town. Confusingly, it is often referred to as Playa Blanca, the same name as a quite separate resort at the southern tip of the island. On the beach side of the Avenida there's an attractive paved walkway with palm trees and gardens; across the street is a long strip of bars and restaurants, bright lights, tourist shops and places of entertainment. After dark, the Centro Atlantico along here is the place to find clubs and nightlife. The tourist office can be found beside the beach. The waterside promenade continues all the way to Pocillos and Matagor beaches.

INFORMATION

➕ C4
✉ Alongside Avenida de las Playas in the western half of town, Puerto del Carmen
🍴 Restaurants (£) on Avenida de las Playas
🚌 Buses from Arrecife approx every half hour

The boards and sails of windsurfers are laid out on the beach in preparation for some adventure on the water

Teguise

INFORMATION

🞥 D3

✉ 9km north of Arrecife

🍴 La Galeria (£), 8 Calle
Nueva (➤ 68)

🚌 No 7, seven times daily to
and from Arrecife. Most
tour operators run weekly
coach trips to Teguise
market on Sunday
morning

🛈 Avenida Gen Franco,
Arrecife (☎ 928 81 37
92)

❓ Festivals at Teguise: 5 Jan
(Cabalgata de los Reyes
Magos); 16 Jul (Fiesta de
Nuestra Señora del
Carmen); 8 Sep (Fiesta de
Nuestra Señora de
Guadalupe)

Lanzarote's former capital is today barely more than a village, but it still has the island's most elegant buildings and greatest charm.

Until 1852 this tiny town was Lanzarote's capital, in the centre of the island, out of reach of the coast's raiders and pirates. Founded in the 15th century by Maciot de Béthencourt, nephew of Lanzarote's Norman conqueror Jean de Béthencourt, it stands on the native islanders' ancient meeting point, known as Acatife. Locals still regard this as the island's real capital, while Arrecife remains *el puerto*, the port.

Though small, Teguise has an airy, confident Iberian colonial style with a handsome square, a grid of narrow cobbled streets and a church. For a hundred years it remained the Canaries' most important town, home of European nobility – the de Béthencourts, the Herreras and others – and gave birth to much Canarian folk culture, including its unique instrument, the timple.

In the white lanes and pleasant plazas of Teguise today, many buildings still possess a certain splendour. In the main square is the ancient, white-capped landmark church, Iglesia de Nuestra Señora de Guadalupe, and the impressive Renaissance mansion Palacio de Spinola (or Espiñola), former home of a wealthy 18th-century Genoese merchant, now a museum. The savings bank Caja de Canarios occupies a 15th-century tithe barn.

In the charming, smaller Plaza 18 Julio, the old hospital dates from 1473, and the snow-white, balconied Casa Cuartel, once an army barracks, from the 17th century. The two conventual churches, the Franciscans' 16th-century San Francisco and Dominicans' 17th-century San Domingo, are a short walk away.

Thousands of people arrive every Sunday for the morning market (➤ 76).

Detail of an arched doorway set in the whitewashed walls of a building in Teguise

Valle de la Geria

The extraordinary vineyards in this blackened landscape are dramatic evidence of the interplay between nature's power and man's creativity.

It might seem unlikely that a blasted rocky terrain covered with grey volcanic debris would be among the most intriguing and even beautiful of landscapes. At first sight, the land appears hostile, barren and bleak. In places the ground has been shattered by volcanic activity, sliced and patterned by deep narrow fissures. Deep under the solid surface, molten lava is still moving.

However, look carefully. Tiny white and coloured living specks dot the dark volcanic stones – miniscule lichens and tiny succulents. Unexpected dips and hollows harbour little clusters of lush natural greenery. In spring the roadsides are lined with wild flowers, some strikingly coloured, like the purple poppies.

Most remarkable are the vineyards, each vine growing deep in a separate hollow dug into the shingly rock. Each hollow shelters behind its own semicircular rock wall. This gives the vines just enough shade and shelter to survive, and catch what little moisture can be gathered through dew and condensation. So successful is the method that each produces some 200kg of grapes in a season. Though cleverly functional, the rows of little horseshoe walls look more like art than agriculture: César Manrique's 'landscape as art' has here become 'farming as geometry'. The vines produce Malvasia grapes, and the wine they make – fresh, dry whites with a rich, pleasant flavour – can be tasted and bought at the various *bodegas* (wine cellars) off the Uga–Masdache road and in Uga.

When stopping to explore, remember that the cutting edges of the rough, sharp, brittle black rocks and stones make walking difficult, and can destroy a pair of shoes in minutes.

INFORMATION

➕ C3

✉ East of Uga; along the Uga to Masdache road (LZ30)

🚹 Playa Grande, Puerto del Carmen (☎ 928 51 53 37)

🔁 Yaiza (➤ 48), Timanfaya National Park (➤ 52)

❓ Wine-growers' *bodegas* such as El Grifo and Bodegas Mozaga offer wine-tasting

Yaiza

INFORMATION

➕ B3

✉ 15km from Playa Blanca, around 20km from Arrecife

🚌 No 6 (Arrecife–Playa Blanca)

♿ Few

↔ Timanfaya National Park (➤ 52), Islote de Hilario (➤ 34), Uga (➤ 51), La Geria (➤ 47)

La Era Restaurant (➤ 69)

✉ Carretera General

☎ 928 83 00 16

🕐 1–4, 7–11

Galería Yaiza

✉ On the Playa Blanca road

☎ 928 83 01 99

🕐 Mon–Sat 5–7. Closed Sun

This arty, yet unpretentious and picturesque old village of palm trees and dazzling whiteness, is often described as one of the Canaries' prettiest.

It is dramatically located, facing golden hills one way, barren blackness the other. Standing on the very edge of the *malpaís*, it was all but destroyed in the Timanfaya volcanic eruptions of 1730–36. Just a handful of houses survived, but, as many surrounding fields and gardens were left intact, villagers slowly returned and rebuilt their homes.

The sunshine reflects brilliantly off their simple whitewashed walls and houses. Some of the homes look prosperous and dignified, with little balconies and pleasing, flower-filled gardens. César Manrique wanted the whole island to look like this.

Accordingly, he set about his favourite task – providing visitors with a good, stylish restaurant. He selected one of the pre-eruption survivals, a 300-year-old farm called La Era, and transformed it into a beautiful and fascinating complex of buildings and outbuildings. Enter through a pretty little green-doored gateway into a quiet courtyard, off which a bar, a shop and gardens form part of his restoration. The main area is a set of small rooms with white walls, and tables laid with attractive, loosely woven gingham cloth. The food is all Canarian specialities, and the crisp, tasty wine is made on the farm. But even if you aren't hungry, it's worth pausing to have a look inside this Manrique restoration.

While in the village, pop into the 18th-century church whose tower rises over the main square, Plaza de los Remedios, and visit the municipal art gallery at the Casa de Cultura or the Galería Yaiza art gallery. The latter exhibits local paintings and ceramics, and most of the work on show is for sale.

LANZAROTE & FUERTEVENTURA's
best

49

Towns & Villages

CARNIVAL ISLANDS

Carnaval brings two weeks of music, dancing, noise, parades, craziness and energy, which on Lanzarote is held mainly on the waterside promenades of Arrecife and Puerto del Carmen. It ends on Ash Wednesday with the zany ceremony of the Burial of the Sardine. For this farcical finale, black-clad mourners sob as a tiny coffin containing the sardine is buried on the seashore. The festival may be less grandiose on Fuerteventura, but has the advantage of being held at several places all over the island. Small towns and villages will put on their own days of colourful, enthusiastic parades and processions, including a day devoted to the Childrens' Carnival.

The whitewashed buildings of El Cotillo, a small fishing village

ANTIGUA (FUERTEVENTURA)

Antigua dates back to 1485 and the early colonial period. The 200-year-old El Molino (windmill), on the main road heading north from the village, has been restored and converted into a cultural and craft centre. Further south at Tiscamanita is another mill and an interpretive centre, the Centro de Interpretación de los Molinos (☎ 928 85 14 00).

➕ IFC ✉ 21km southwest of Puerto del Rosario ▮▮ El Molino de Antigua (££) ☎ 928 87 84 82 🚌 No 1 from Puerto del Rosario to Morro del Jable six times daily ♿ None ↔ Betancuría (➤ 25) ❓ 8 Sep is the Fiesta of Our Lady of Antigua

CALETA DE FUSTES (FUERTEVENTURA)

This popular, fast-growing resort area receives large numbers of package tourists. There's a very good golden beach, a few lively bars and several inexpensive eating places. An 18th-century fortified round tower of dark stone, called simply El Castillo – the castle – stands next to a little pleasure harbour and has become part of a beach complex with restaurants, bars, watersports hire facilities and a supermarket.

➕ IFC ✉ 12km south of Puerto del Rosario ▮▮ Selection of restaurants (£–££) 🚌 No 3 from Puerto del Rosario to Caleta de Fustes

COSTA TEGUISE

What this resort lacks in history or character is made up for by a location ideal for sun, sea, sand, sport and sightseeing. In addition to the main, long, sandy Las Cucharas beach there are other enjoyable waterfront areas, including watersports facilities and an aquapark. To the north of the town is an 18-hole golf course.

➕ E3 ✉ On the coast 7km northwest of Arrecife ▮▮ Beachside bar-restaurants (££) 🚌 No 1 from Arrecife ♿ Good ↔ Arrecife (➤ 24), Fundación César Manrique (➤ 30)

EL COTILLO (FUERTEVENTURA)

This small holiday development around a fishing harbour on the windy west coast near La Oliva has black cliffs, sandy beaches, watersports and an 18th-century fortification called the Torre del Tostón or Castillo de Rico Roque.

➕ IFC ✉ 20km south of Corralejo ▮▮ Simple restaurants (£) near the harbour 🚌 No 8 to Corralejo every two hours; No 7 to Puerto del Rosario ↔ Antigua (➤ above), Corralejo (➤ 26)

FEMÉS

This likeable, secret little village on the back road to
Playa Blanca was one of the first European
settlements on the island, and the village church of
San Marcial de Rubicón was the first cathedral to be
built in the Canary Islands .

🔲 B4 ✉ 5km south of Uga; 8km north of Playa Blanca 🍴 Several
restaurants (£–££) in Playa Blanca 🚌 No 5 from Femés to Arrecife
once daily Mon–Fri 🔄 Playa Blanca (➤ 44), Papagayo (➤ 43), Uga
(➤ below)

HARÍA

A delightful little town in a lush green valley.
The narrow streets and lanes are speckled with
colour where purple bougainvillaea and red
pelargoniums climb brilliant white walls.

🔲 E2 ✉ 15km north of Teguise 🍴 Snack bars (£) on the southern
edge of town; Restaurante El Cortijo (££) serves classic Lanzarote dishes
🚌 No 7 from Arrecife; the journey takes about 1 hour 🔄 Mirador del
Rio (➤ 39) ❓ Fiesta de San Juan celebrates midsummer on 24 Jun

ORZOLA

This little working fishing harbour makes a good base
for keen anglers, while for those who would rather eat
a fish than catch one, it's also an excellent lunch stop.
There are good beaches nearby, too.

🔲 E1 ✉ 37km north of Arrecife 🍴 Restaurante Punta Fariones
(££), just off the harbour 🚌 No 9 from Arrecife at 7:40AM daily. Leaves
Orzola for Arrecife at about 4:30PM ⛴ Ferries at 10AM and 4PM to
Graciosa (➤ 32) 🔄 El Mirador del Rio (➤ 39), Isla Graciosa
(➤ 32), Cueva de los Verdes (➤ 28), Jameos del Agua (➤ 35)

PÁJARA (FUERTEVENTURA)

The parish church of Our Lady of Regla is architect-
urally one of Fuerteventura's most important historic
buildings. The village itself is shady and enticing.

🔲 IFC ✉ 40km southwest of Puerto del Rosario 🍴 Bars (£) in the
village 🚌 Nos 4 and 9 from Jandia twice daily ♿ None
🔄 Hermitage of Our Lady of Peña (➤ 59)

OLD HARBOUR, PUERTO DEL CARMEN

The small fishing harbour was the heart of the
original Puerto del Carmen village. It's still very
much in use today; in the square next to the port you
can watch the locals playing boules.

🔲 C4 ✉ Western edge of town 🍴 Seafood places (£) surround the
harbour 🚌 Buses from Arrecife stop on Avenida de las Playas ♿ Few

UGA

An incongruously green and fertile wine village on
the fringes of the desolate volcanic terrain of the
Timanfaya National Park, Uga stands at the western
end of the bizzare La Geria vineyard area, where the
wine bushes grow in volcanic rubble.

🔲 B3 ✉ 17km west of Arrecife 🍴 Gregorio (££) is a traditional
island inn 🚌 No 6 (Arrecife–Playa Blanca) ♿ Few 🔄 Yaiza (➤ 48),
La Geria (➤ 47), Timanfaya National Park (➤ 52)

*Flowers and palm trees
in the courtyard before
the gleaming white
façade of the church in
the village of Uga*

In Timanfaya National Park

HOW VOLCANOES WORK

Inside the earth, rock is a boiling liquid called magma. Where the surface crust is weak or broken, magma sometimes forces its way out through long hollows called pipes. Bursting out as solids, liquids and gases, it builds deposits into a volcanic cone. Eruptions can also break out of a volcano's sides or blow gases through underground tunnels.

Unlike most of the world's national parks, at first sight this one has no animal life, no birdlife, and not a blade of grass, flower or shrub growing anywhere. Instead the eye must become accustomed to a vast landscape of twisted and convoluted devastation. A stylised devil is the symbol of the park. With his horns, tail and trident, he conjures up a sense of mischief and fun, but while the Mountains of Fire may be fun to visit, they are a serious power. There are 36 volcanic cones within the park's 8sq km, and though they are peaceful enough at the moment, these volcanoes are still active. The black and grey desert of clinker and ash that surrounds the cones is the result of 26 eruptions between 1730 and 1736.

ECHADERO DE LOS CAMELLOS (CAMEL PARK)

Lanzarote's camels are actually dromedaries, but nobody's quibbling over what is really just an

amusement for tourists. The camel park is a corral at the foot of Timanfaya, where visitors can wait in line for a 10-minute ride up the steep, unstable slag heap of the volcano. Each animal carries two passengers, who are strapped into wooden seats, one perched on either side of the camel. The camel train is then led up the slope by a guide.

✚ B3 ✉ 3km north of Yaiza, at the foot of Timanfaya/Islote de Hilario
🕐 Daily 9–4 🍴 El Diablo restaurant (££) at the summit ⬌ Isolote de Hilario (► 34), Mancha Blanca Centro de Interpretacion (► 38)

A camel 'train' returning from the Parque Nacional de Timanfaya where they take vistors around the park

MONTAÑA RAJADA

Only to be seen on the Ruta de los Volcanes bus tour, this 350m peak gives one of the most awe-inspiring views of the park: a panoramic vista over volcanic cones and craters and the hollows caused by underground tunnels collapsing. Beyond, the blue sea makes a startling contrast.

✚ B3 ✉ 2km southwest of Islote de Hilario ⬌ On Ruta de los Volcanes coach tour (► 17)

MONTAÑA DE TIMANFAYA

This, the largest of the park's volcanoes at 510m, is a vast dark cone that dominates the view throughout western Lanzarote. You can see it up close and admire

the vivid red and yellow streaks (caused by mineral deposits) on the Volcanoes coach tour.

🞦 B3 ✉ 1km southwest of Islote de Hilario 🚌 On Ruta de los Volcanes coach tour (➤ 17)

The desolate landscape of the Parque Nacional de Timanfaya

PLAYA DE LA MADERA

Where the park meets the sea there are inaccessible coves and black sand beaches. One of these can be reached by car on a track that is marked – very truthfully – Camino en Mal Estado ('track in poor condition'). The track can be reached from Tinajo, Mancha Blanca or a turn close to the Islote de Hilario entrance.

🞦 B3 ✉ 10km northwest of Mancha Blanca 🚌 None

Lichen colonising the volcanic rock surface of Montaña de las Lapas o del Cuervo

TIMANFAYA PLAIN

The flat lowland that lies at the foot of the volcanoes is a sea of dark jagged rock, resembling the burnt out clinker after a coal fire. The terrain is so unusual that it deserves a good look.

🞦 B3 ✉ Between Yaiza and park entrance

VALLE DE LA TRANQUILIDAD (VALLEY OF TRANQUILLITY)

In this part of the park some tiny bushes are trying to grow and a few tufts of grey-looking grasses manage to cling to the slopes, a hint of the future greenery that may one day take hold here.

🞦 B3 ✉ 1km south of Islote de Hilario 🚌 On Ruta de los Volcanes coach tour (➤ 17)

Beaches

FAMILY FRIENDLY

Lanzarote and Fuerteventura claim to offer the most wonderful beaches in Europe. Some of the best choices for families with children on Lanzarote are Caleton Blanca, Papagayo and Playa Grande. On Fuerteventura parents usually choose the Corralejo Dunes and Sotavento beach on the Jandía Peninsula.

PLAYA DE COFETE AND PLAYA BARLOVENTO 'WINDWARD' (FUERTEVENTURA)

On the western side of Jandía there are vast empty sands. The beaches are difficult to reach in anything other than all-terrain vehicles, but those who make it will be rewarded. Swimming is not recommended due to the wind and undercurrents.

➕ IFC ✉ 80km south of Puerto del Rosario 🍴 Several restaurants (£) 🚌 No 1 from Puerto del Rosario to Morro del Jable via all eastern Jandia resorts (▶ 36)

CALETON BLANCA

Warm and sheltered. The swimming is safe here and there are rock pools to explore.

➕ E1 ✉ 1km south of Orzola

PLAYA DE LAS CONCHAS

Found on Isla Graciosa, off Lanzarote, this is a spectacular beach of black rock and golden sand. Be careful when swimming as there are strong currents just offshore in the deeper waters.

➕ E1 ✉ From Orzola at 10AM, back to Orzola at 4PM

PLAYAS DE CORRALEJO (FUERTEVENTURA)

A very good golden sand beach 10km long and backed by huge dunes. Beyond the dunes are wonderful views to the mountains. There are small white sand beaches near the fishing port in town.

➕ IFC ✉ Corralejo 30km north of Puerto del Rosario 🍴 Several restaurants (£) 🚌 No 6 via Puerto del Rosario and No 7 via La Oliva

PLAYA DORADA

A delightful sandy beach shelving into a sheltered bay, perfect for swimming and sunbathing.

➕ B4 ✉ Playa Blanca

FAMARA

So good that visitors are prepared to put up with the slightly more temperamental weather and that little bit of extra wind that comes from the northwest. The ocean currents are also more dangerous here, so swimming and diving are discouraged.

➕ D2 ✉ 11km north of Teguise 🍴 Several restaurants (£) 🚌 No 18 runs once a day, from La Caleta to Arrecife in the morning and back to La Caleta in the evening 🔄 Haria (▶ 51), Mirador del Rio (▶ 39)

PLAYA DE LA GARITA

Tucked away and popular with those in search of an escape, this 400m long natural beach is particularly clean. A few shops and a children's playground.

🔢 E2 ✉ Arrieta 🚌 4 times daily from Arrecife

PLAYA DE LOS POCILLOS, PUERTO DEL CARMEN

With a vast, sandy beach 2km from the centre of town, Pocillos is much quieter and less crowded, with some above-average accommodation. The northern end of Pocillos beach is an appealing stretch with good restaurants and shops, called Los Jameos Playa. Popular with families.

🔢 D4 🍴 Restaurants (£) at Los Jameos Playa 🚌 Buses from Arrecife approx every half hour

PLAYA DE MATAGORDA, PUERTO DEL CARMEN

Farthest from town and very near the airport runway, Playa Matagorda has fewer attractions and feels remote, yet is sandy and has a couple of good hotels. The beach is almost completely covered at high tide. Surfing station.

🔢 D4 🚌 Buses into Puerto del Carmen and Arrecife every half hour 🍴 Restaurants in Centro Commerciales

COSTA TEGUISE

There are two beaches here. The main stretch, Las Cucharas, is long and sandy. The towns second beach is also sandy, but with a rocky foreshore. Watersports facilities are available at both.

🔢 E3 ✉ On the coast 7km northwest of Arrecife 🍴 High-quality beachside bar-restaurants (££) on Playa de las Cucharas 🚌 No 1 from Arrecife every half an hour throughout the day Mon—Fri, every hour at weekends and festivals. Journey takes 20 minutes ♿ Good ↔ Arrecife (► 24), Fundación César Manrique (► 30)

Holidaymakers crowd the sands of Playa de las Cucharas

For Children

Many of the sights thrill kids every bit as much as grown-ups. The sights most likely to appeal to the younger generation are listed here.

LANZAROTE

ARRIETA
CUEVA DE LOS VERDES
The haunting music and lighting combine to make a visit to this fascinating cave system a magical experience for children (➤ 28).
☎ 928 17 32 20 🕐 Regular tours daily 10–5

JAMEOS DEL AGUA
Spotting the tiny blind white crabs, the amazing auditorium in a cave, and – most of all – the Casa de los Volcanes hands-on science museum at the top of the cliff will fascinate and amuse any child (➤ 35).
☎ 928 84 80 20 🕐 Daily 9:30–6:45; Tue, Fri, Sat open till 3am

COSTA TEGUISE
AQUA PARK
This water park has fantastic, colourful waterslides and flumes, lovely heated swimming pools and sunloungers and shaded areas for the grown-ups. Kids aged 2–12 pay reduced price, over 12s full price.
✉ 2km inland from Costa Teguise ☎ 928 59 21 28
🕐 Daily 10–6 (10–5 in winter)

GUATIZA
JARDÍN DE CACTUS
Is that cactus real? Especially the giant cactus outside? Go and see. One thing is for certain, the 1,400 varieties inside the garden are definitely genuine and very weird (➤ 37).

GUINATE
PARQUE TROPICAL
Little ones will enjoy this bird world where some 300 species of birds can be seen and there are regular shows by performing parrots.
☎ 928 83 55 00 🕐 Daily 10–5

PUERTO DEL CARMEN
BLUE DELFIN
Variety of trips and mini-cruises daily, plus free bus transfers.
☎ 928 51 23 23

SUBMARINE SAFARIS AND TOURS
Journey in a real submarine, with high-tech viewing options. A choice of companies.
✉ Puerto Calero ☎ 928 51 28 98; 928 51 00 65; 928 73 12 93

The well-landscaped Jardin de Cactus

GRAN KARTING CLUB

Lanzarote's go-karting track. Karts come in all sizes to suit adults as well as children. The site also has a bar, cafeteria and playground. A fun family outing.

✉ La Rinconada, Arrecife road ☎ 619 75 99 46 🕙 Daily, summer 11–10; winter 10–9

TARO DE TAHÍCHE
FUNDACIÓN CÉSAR MANRIQUE

Children will be entranced by the house Manrique made for himself, especially the underground rooms in spherical lava bubbles (➤ 30). The adults will be fascinated too.

MANRIQUE MOBILES

Manrique's mischievous, childlike inventiveness strikes a chord with the youngest art-lovers when they see his mad mobiles, standing at junctions and roundabouts like giant coloured toys turning, whirling and whizzing in the wind. See if you can spot the one at the airport as soon as you arrive in Lanzarote.

TIMANFAYA
ISLOTE DE HILARIO

Only the youngest or weariest of children could fail to be astonished by the fire and water magic at the hottest spot on the volcanic island (➤ 34). There are camel rides at the Echerado de los Camellos (➤ 52).

FUERTEVENTURA

CORRALEJO
CARNAVAL

A dazzling show, for two weeks in February or March, which allows wild behaviour. Failing that, enjoy the crazy noise, colour and flamboyance of any local fiesta. During the fortnight some time will be devoted to a children's carnival.

CATAMARÁN CELIA CRUZ

Boat trips to Lobos Island and Corralejo beaches.
☎ 616 99 22 43 🕙 Mon, Tue, Wed, 12AM–1:30PM

LAJITA
ZOO SAFARI DE CAMELLOS

The main attraction of this small zoo park is a 30-minute ride on one of its herd of 250 dromedaries. Ponies and donkeys are also available for rides. Toucans, cranes, parrots, pelicans and ostriches are the most spectacular of its 200 species of birds and there are also lizards and crocodiles. You can buy exotic flora at the garden centre.
☎ 928 16 11 35 🕙 Daily 9–7

CHILDREN WELCOME

The islanders, like other Spaniards, never make kids feel excluded. It's a sign, perhaps, of their affection for children, that restaurants, bars and cafés don't generally list children's menus or portions. Instead, children are warmly welcomed, indulged, given little portions and allowed into any establishment at any hour of the day or night.

LATE NIGHTS

Your children will be quick to notice one Spanish custom they'll want to follow on holiday: there is no bedtime. Spanish families can often be seen out as late as midnight, having dinner or going for a stroll together. Restaurants think nothing of catering for children in the evening. Even at home, children are often up playing while the grown-ups talk until late. It's taken for granted that children are a constant part of family life.

Free Attractions

CASTILLO DE LAS COLORADAS

The restored circular watchtower called Castillo de las Coloradas (or Torre del Águila – Aguila Tower) stands guard beside the beach at Aguila where de Béthencourt is said to have made his first landing on Lanzarote in 1402. In actual fact he had already dropped anchor in El Río and stepped on to the island of Graciosa. Another local story is that de Béthencourt himself erected the tower, though in fact it was built much later; it bears the date of 1769, and it is thought most of the present structure is even later, dating from 1778. There are good views from here across the straits to Fuerteventura.

➕ B4 ✉ Playa Blanca, Aguila 🚌 Playa Blanca (➤ 44)

CASTILLO DE SAN GABRIEL

Poised on a tiny islet called Islote de los Ingleses, just

off the main town centre old harbour, Castillo de San Gabriel adds charm to Arrecife's waterfront. Built in 1590 by Italian architect Leonardo Torriani on part of the string of rocky islets off the town, the castle became a vital part of the defences protecting the harbour and town from marauding pirates.

➕ c3 ✉ Avenida Gen Franco, Arrecife ☎ 928 80 28 84 🕐 Tue–Fri 10–1, 4–7, Sat 10–1 🍴 Cafés (£) in Calle Leon y Castillo 🚌 From Avenida Gen Franco 🚻 Few 🅿 Free

The causeway which links the city centre of Arrecife to the Castillo de San Gabriel beyond

CENTRO DE ARTE Y CULTURA AFRICANA

On the waterfront at Arrieta stands the astonishing blue and red house (within a walled garden) of the Centro de Arte y Cultura Africana (Museum of African Art and Culture), celebrating the connection between the Canaries and the nearby continent.

➕ E2 ✉ On waterfront, Arrieta ☎ None 🕐 Daily 10:30–6:30. Closed Sun 🚻 Few 🅿 Free

EL CHARCO DE SAN GINÉS

This curious little lake or lagoon of sea water, surrounded by a walkway and modest fishermen's cottages, is said to lie at the very origin of Arrecife. The legendary San Ginés lived here as a hermit beside the water. A village of pious fishing folk grew around the hermitage, and as the village expanded into a town, the hermitage became the town's church.

➕ c2 ✉ Avenida Vargos, Arrecife 🍴 Cafés (£) on waterfront 🚌 From Avenida Gen Franco 🚻 Few 🅿 Free

ERMITA DE LOS DOLORES
(HERMITAGE OF THE SORROWS)
Pilgrims flock to this beautiful church in Mancha Blanca, especially on 15 September, the feast day of the Virgin of the Volcanoes. The village stands above the desolate *malpaís* at the point where it meets neatly farmed, highly productive fields layered with *picón*.

➕ C3 ✉ Mancha Blanca ⏰ Open all day every day; locked at night 🍴 Bar-restaurant (££) across the road 💷 Donations welcome
🔄 Islote de Hilario (➤ 34), Timanfaya National Park (➤ 52)
❓ Processions and celebrations on the Fiesta de la Virgen de los Volcanes, every year on 15 Sep

ERMITA DE NUESTRA SEÑORA DE LA PEÑA
(FUERTEVENTURA)
Tucked away in the hills outside Vega de Rio Palmas, this tiny white building houses an alabaster statue of the revered patron saint of Fuerteventura. The third Saturday in September is her feast day, which brings crowds of islanders here for the all-important *romería*, the fascinating annual pilgrimage and procession

➕ IFC ✉ 5km south of Betancuria on the Pájara road ⏰ Tue–Sat 11–1 and 5–7. Closed Sun and Mon 🚌 No 2 from Puerto del Rosario to Vega Rio Palma twice daily 🔄 Betancuria (➤ 25), Pájara (➤ 51)

LOS HERVIDEROS
On the western shore, where the dark volcanic *malpaís* descends into the blue Atlantic waves, a *mirador* (viewpoint) looks across at a place where the ocean thunders in and out of sea caverns. The turbulent, bubbling effect has been called Los Hervideros, the boiling waters.

➕ B3 ✉ 3km off the Yaiza to Playa Blanca road 🍴 Nearby restaurants (£) in El Golfo, Janubio or Yaiza 🔄 El Golfo (➤ 31), Yaiza (➤ 48), Timanfaya National Park (➤ 52)

IGLESIA DE SAN GINÉS
Arrecife's main church, this dignified little building of dark volcanic stone and bright white paintwork is dedicated to the town's patron saint. Built in the 18th century and now handsomely restored, the church is still at the old heart of the town, standing at one end of a pleasant square.

➕ c2 ✉ Plaza de San Ginés, Arrecife ⏰ Open to public daily 9–1, 5–7 except during church services 🚌 From Avenida Gen Franco 🚫 None
💷 Free ❓ Annual Fiesta de San Ginés in August brings processions, parades and traditional dancing to the streets

MONUMENTO A DON MIGUEL DE UNAMUNO
(FUERTEVENTURA)
At the foot of the volcanic Montaña Quemada, in the hills south of La Oliva, a monument records the exile to Fuerteventura of Miguel de Unamuno (1864–1936), the poet and thinker.

➕ IFC ✉ Near the junction of Route 600 and Route 610
🚌 No 2 (Puerto del Rosario to Vega Rio Palma) 🚫 None
🔄 La Oliva (➤ 42)

Surf washes over the rocks as the waves come crashing into an inlet through the black volcanic rock coastline of Los Hervideros

59

Places to Have Lunch

CASA MIGUEL (£)
Quayside restaurant at the often-overlooked coastal town of Arrieta that serves good home cooking.
✉ Arrieta Harbour ☎ 928 83 52 25

CASTILLO DE SAN JOSÉ (££)
The restaurant of Lanzarote's modern art gallery, inside an oceanside 15th-century fortress, is a typical example of César Manrique's imaginative style.
✉ Castillo de San José, Arrecife ☎ 928 81 23 21

EL DIABLO (££)
Bright, busy focal point at the summit of Islote de Hilario (▶ 34). Panoramic views, and good traditional cuisine cooked over heat rising from the earth.
✉ Timanfaya National Park ☎ 928 84 00 57

LA ERA (££)
Stylish yet rustic restaurant and bar in a 300-year-old Yaiza farm restored by César Manrique. House wine from their own vineyards.
✉ Carretera General, Yaiza. The restaurant lies back off the road, and is signposted ☎ 928 83 00 16

LA GALERÍA (£)
Relaxed, characterful place serving tapas, a range of fish dishes, stews and desserts.
✉ 8 Calle Nueva, Teguise (by main square) ☎ 928 84 50 44

LOS HELECHOS (£)
At this restaurant you can feast on the superb view as much as the fresh fish and popular dishes.
✉ At the viewpoint 5km south of Haría ☎ 928 83 50 89

LA MARQUESINA (££)
At the harbour. Relaxed and unpretentious place popular with locals. Fresh fish a speciality.
✉ Muelle Viejo, Corralejo, Fuerteventura ☎ 928 53 54 35

MESÓN LA JORDANA (££)
La Jordana gives a local flavour to some international favourites.
✉ Calle Los Geranios, Costa Teguise ☎ 928 59 03 28

EL MOLINO DE ANTIGUA (££)
A restored 200-year-old windmill just outside Antigua offers tasty local dishes in a rustic setting.
✉ El Molino, Antigua, Fuerteventura ☎ 927 87 82 20

PUNTA FARIONES (£)
In a neat blue and white building by the little harbour, this modest restaurant serves fresh fish and seafood.
✉ Calle La Quemadita, Orzola ☎ 928 84 25 58

The Restaurant La Era, converted by the artist César Manrique in 1970, is housed within one of only three houses in Yaiza which survived the massive volcanic eruptions of 1730–36

LANZAROTE & FUERTEVENTURA
where to...

EAT AND DRINK

STAY

SHOP

BE ENTERTAINED

Lanzarote

PRICES

Prices are approximate, based on a three-course meal for one, without drinks and service:

£   = under 12 euros
££   = 12–18 euros
£££ = over 18 euros

MEALS WITH A VIEW

Lanzarote has a number of restaurants with great views, including Castillo de San Jose (► 62), Los Cascajos and Mirador de la Valle (both ► 65). But for food and drink with an in-flight panorama don't miss Mirador del Río (► 65).

ARRECIFE

Campañitas (£)

A typical Spanish cafeteria in the commercial centre near the ring road, ideal for a drink, snack or a complete meal if you're shopping or exploring.

✉ Via Medular ☎ 928 81 19 19 🕐 8:30AM–9:30PM

Castillo de San José (££)

Inside the Castillo, attached to the modern art museum and facing the sea through a panoramic window, this restaurant was designed by César Manrique as a work of art itself. There are black walls, black tables, even black napkins, and modern classical music playing. The food is sophisticated and well presented, with a moderately priced menu of the day. Can be visited without going to the museum.

✉ Museo Internacional de Arte Contemporaneo, Castillo de San José , Carretera de Puerto Naos (3km north of Arrecife on main Costa Teguise road) ☎ 928 81 23 21 🕐 1PM–3:45PM and 8PM–11PM. Bar 11AM–1AM

Ciao (£)

Across the road from the sea at the start of the waterside gardens. The big, cool tiled interior of this typical Spanish bar-restaurant offers respite from the heat and noise, though there are also outdoor tables. A wide choice includes a modestly priced three-course meal including wine.

✉ 1 Calle La Esperanza ☎ 928 81 35 11 🕐 All day

El Pajar (££)

An attractive black and white exterior (and similar interior) of whitewash and volcanic stone compensates for a main-road setting opposite the landmark Gran Hotel tower. Paellas and pizzas are served as well as local meat, fish and seafood specialities and home-made desserts. Excellent value.

✉ 48 Avenida Mancomunidad ☎ 928 81 54 95 🕐 Lunch, dinner

Hotel Lancelot (££)

The restaurant of this pleasant hotel facing Arrecife's sandy beach is open to the public for very reasonable international cooking.

✉ 9 Avenida Mancomunidad ☎ 928 80 50 90 🕐 Lunch, dinner

Los Troncos (££)

This much praised shellfish and fish restaurant by the Naos port has interesting meat and fish dishes as well as well-known favourites.

✉ 9 Calle Agustin de la Hoz, Arrecife ☎ 928 81 36 37 🕐 Lunch, dinner

ARRIETA

Casa Miguel (£)

This quayside restaurant in a simple little blue and white building at this often-overlooked harbour near Jameos del Agua serves good, unpretentious home cooking.

✉ Calle La Noria, La Garita ☎ 928 83 52 25 🕐 Lunch, dinner. Closed Mon

El Charcón (££)

Popular bar-restaurant on the quayside. Adjacent is a small cove where children can play safely while waiting for traditional dishes, which take a little longer, to be prepared.

✉ **Calle La Noria, La Garita**
🕐 **All day**

Jameos del Agua (££)

When César Manrique turned this bizarre volcanic feature into a major tourist attraction, he added snack bars and a restaurant serving good Canarian cuisine. There could hardly be a stranger place to eat.

✉ **Jameos del Agua, beside sea near Arrieta (Haría district)** ☎ **928 83 50 10** 🕐 **Snack bars open all day; restaurant Tue, Fri, Sat 7PM–3AM (folklore show 11PM)**

El Lago (££)

10 minutes' walk from the town centre along the shore road, the restaurant has a fine view and offers a range of shellfish, fish and meat dishes.

✉ **On seafront north of harbour** ☎ **928 84 81 76** 🕐 **Mon–Sat 12–10, Sun 12–5**

LA CALETA DE FAMARA

Bajamar Casa Garcia (£)

Simple, satisfying little place, adorned with green trellis, hanging plants and check oilcloth tablecovers. The food is a tasty mix of local and European.

✉ **Famara road** ☎ **928 52 85 76** 🕐 **All day**

Las Bajas (£)

Basic, but popular, meat and fish dishes, both inter-national and local, are served at this simple but charming eating place located on the edge of a genuine fishing village.

✉ **Calle Callejon** ☎ **928 52 85 49** 🕐 **Lunch, dinner**

Casa Ramon (£)

Many visitors pause here for a simple, unpretentious Spanish lunch.

✉ **Calle Callejon** 🕐 **Lunch, dinner**

COSTA TEGUISE

Bernardo's (££)

Attractively fitted out with various shades of green cane chairs and glass-topped tables, this fish-oriented restaurant makes a pleasant open-air place for lunch next to the main beach. Enjoy *sama* (a local fish) in white wine sauce.

✉ **Centro Comercial Las Cucharas** 🕐 **All day**

Casa Blanca (££)

In a charming little detached building with a hexagonal roof, this unusual grill restaurant in the Jablillo area has a kitchen open to view and dark wooden tables on an enclosed terrace. Local fish dishes, salads and steak with peppercorns are among the choices.

✉ **4 Calle las Olas** ☎ **928 59 01 55** 🕐 **Dinner**

La Chimenea (££)

Good Italian food at the main beach. Relaxing décor of cool green and white motif outside, warmer orange inside.

✉ **Centro Comercial Las Cucharas** ☎ **928 59 08 37** 🕐 **Lunch, dinner. Closed Sun**

RESTAURANTE MANRIQUE

Several restaurants designed by César Manrique are based on a similar he concept: a wide, low structure of sweeping curves, made of volcanic rock, with a panoramic window. But despite the similarities, each is styled to capture the sense of its location. And Manrique thought of every detail. Not only did he personally design the toilets at his sites, but even the rubbish bins were specially adapted for their particular place.

COSTA TEGUISE RESTAURANTS

Costa Teguise is divided into three distinct areas for dining purposes: Playa de las Cucharas, in the north of the resort; the busier area around Playa del Jabillo (including Plaza Pueblo Martinero); and the smaller Playa Bastian area at the southern end of town. There is a short drive between each of these three districts, and taxis ply between them constantly.

Columbus Tavern (££)

Catering for thoroughly British tastes, this laid-back bar-restaurant offers salads, spaghetti bolognese and home-made puddings – plus a lovely view of the main beach.

✉ **Centro Commercial Las Cucharas** ☎ **928 59 20 16** ⏰ **All day**

Doña Lola (£)

Looking along the coast towards Arrecife, the terrace of this unassuming café-bar is a lovely place to enjoy a drink or a meal from an extensive menu of classic Spanish and international dishes.

✉ **Centro Commercial Jablillo** ☎ **608 01 13 28** ⏰ **All day**

La Graciosa, Melía Salinas Hotel (£££)

The smartest hotel on the island has an elegant restaurant open to the public. The food is sophisticated, mainly French, with giant prawns, or sole with scallops mousse, but with local dishes too, like fish *à la sal con dos mojos*. Wonderful desserts. Live music.

✉ **Ave de las Islas Canarias** ☎ **928 59 00 40** ⏰ **Dinner. Closed Sun, Mon**

Mesón La Jordana (£££)

One of Costa Teguise's best restaurants, with green and white country-style décor and a menu that gives a local flavour to international cooking. Playa Bastían area.

✉ **Calle Los Geranios** ☎ **928 59 03 28** ⏰ **Lunch, dinner. Closed Sun**

Montmartre (£££)

A neon 'Moulin Rouge' on the roof is a reminder of the real Montmartre, as are the quarry-tiled floor, oil lamps and pink and white tablecloths. Fine French cooking, with duck liver pâté, and chicken stuffed with prawns.

✉ **Ave de las Palmeras, near corner of Calle Geranio** ☎ **928 59 12 05** ⏰ **Dinner. Closed Thu**

Neptuno (££)

Tucked away in a little plaza at the seafront end of Ave. de Jabillo, this relaxed but stylish establishment is favoured by locals rather than tourists. Well prepared fish and seafood dishes.

✉ **Centro Commercial Neptuno, Ave de Jabillo** ☎ **928 59 03 78** ⏰ **Lunch, dinner**

El Patio (£)

A cut above the rest in authenticity, style and the cooking of its Spanish and Canarian dishes. Tables are arranged under a green awning on their own terrace beside a crowded pedestrian square.

✉ **Plaza Pueblo Martinero** ☎ **928 59 09 45** ⏰ **Lunch, dinner**

El Pescador (£)

Alongside a busy pedestrian plaza, this restaurant invites you to come inside and shut out the noise. Good service and an emphasis on seafood, which is reflected by the fish-inspired décor.

✉ **Plaza Pueblo Martinero** ☎ **928 59 08 74** ⏰ **Lunch, dinner**

La Provence (££)

A tasty muddle of Mexican, Italian, Spanish and, yes, some Provençal dishes at this popular grill restaurant.

✉ Avenida del Jablillo
☎ 928 59 22 18
🕐 Lunch, dinner

Vesubio (£)

Offers all the usual Spanish and foreign favourites on a terrace looking across the beach and down the coast towards Arrecife.

✉ Centro Commerical Jablillo ☎ 928 80 46 75
🕐 All day

EL GOLFO

El Golfo (££)

Simple fresh fish and shellfish dishes, as well as the ever-popular paella, between the sea and the *malpaís*.

✉ El Golfo ☎ 928 83 00 89
🕐 Lunch, dinner

GUATIZA

Jardín de Cactus (£)

Beneath the windmill, big wooden tables under a sail-cloth awning. Enjoy a drink or a light meal and gaze at Manrique's amazing cactus collection.

✉ Jardín de Cactus, Guatiza (17km northeast of Arrecife) ☎ 928 52 93 97 🕐 Daily 10–5

HARÍA

Casa Cura (££)

Satisfying Canarian food prepared in an atmospheric old house. Several local stews like *sancocho*, *puchero* and *potaje* served in little dining rooms.

✉ 1 Calle Nueva (right turn off road to Yé and Mirador del Río) ☎ 928 83 55 55 🕐 Lunch, dinner

Los Cascajos (£)

Just out of town to the north, with great valley views, this rustic restaurant has both local and Spanish favourites.

✉ 9 Calle Maria Herera ☎ 928 83 54 71 🕐 Lunch, dinner. Closed Sun

El Cortijo (££)

In an attractive whitewashed converted farmhouse set back from the road, this popular restaurant serves classic Lanzarote dishes.

✉ On the Teguise road, at the edge of the village ☎ 928 83 50 06 🕐 11–8

Los Helechos (£)

At this big canteen-style restaurant you can feast on the superb view as much as the self-service snacks and light meals.

✉ At the viewpoint 5km south of Haría ☎ 928 83 50 89 🕐 10–6

Mirador de la Valle (£)

Enjoy a snack at this simple viewpoint location looking across the Haría valley.

✉ Los Valles, on road south of Haría ☎ 928 52 80 36 🕐 Lunch, dinner. Closed Tue

Mirador del Río (£)

Manrique's starting point when constructing this spectacular site was the restaurant. Drinks, snacks, and an exquisite setting.

✉ About 7km north of Haria ☎ 928 17 35 38 🕐 Daily 10–6

VOLCANIC WINE

Other Spanish wines come cheaper, but do try the local wine, red, rosé and white, the latter being especially good. It's made from *malvasis* (or malmsey) grapes, first brought to Lanzarote from Crete in the Middle Ages. Large-scale cultivation of the grape did not begin until after the Timanfaya eruptions of 1730–36: islanders discovered the grapevine was one of the only plants able to thrive in the volcanic debris. Each bush produces around 200 kilos of grapes per season.

***TAPAS* ONE**

Tapas bars are not a prominent feature of the islands, particularly in the purpose-built modern resorts, but you will find the occasional bona-fide tapas bar in the older parts of town and *tapas* (Spanish snacks) are also available in some traditional drinking bars and restaurants. This may be as informal as a few olives, cheese and a wedge of tortilla (potato omelette) or it can be a whole variety of dishes which combined make up a substantial meal. Some typical tapas are: *chorizo* (spicy salami-style sausage), *boquerones* (anchovies), octopus salad, prawn salad, Russian salad, *albondigas* (meatballs in a tomato sauce) and the ubiquitous *jamon serrano* (cured mountain ham). The latter either hangs from the ceiling or is placed on the counter in a special cradle-like holder ready for slicing.

ISLA GRACIOSA

El Marinero (£)
Fresh fish and local wines are the specialities. It's even possible to pre-book a meal when you use the Romero ferry from Orzola.
✉ Caleta del Sebo
🕐 Lunch, dinner

MOZAGA

Casa Museo del Campesino (££)
Beside the Monument, this attractive Manrique-built farm-style restaurant serves a wide range of traditional dishes, with much use of *gofio*.
✉ San Bartolomé (on road between San Bartolomé and Mozaga) ☎ 928 52 09 33
🕐 Lunch

NAZARET

Lagomar (££)
An extraordinary setting carved into cliffs and connected to the ground by a tunnel and steps, with gardens, caves, a lake and walkways. Imaginative dishes, mainly French and Italian in inspiration.
✉ On main road between Tahiche and Teguise ☎ 928 84 56 65 🕐 Lunch Tue–Sun. Dinner only on Thu, Fri and Sat. Closed Mon

ORZOLA

Bahia de Orzola (£)
Blue and white cloths and paintwork mirror the marine location of this popular fish restaurant right on the dockside.
✉ Avenida de Caleton ☎ 928 84 25 75 🕐 Lunch, dinner

Casa Arraez (£)
Rough red tables made from old rope spools stand on the quay at this place, which looks like a fisherman's shack. The set meal of Canarian stew and dessert, with bread and wine, is a bargain.
✉ At the far end of Avenida de Caleton 🕐 Lunch, dinner

Perla del Atlantico (£)
With a good position on the quayside of this working fishing harbour, this blue and white restaurant serves excellent fresh fish or grilled squid, with desserts that include *bienmesabe*.
✉ Avenida de Caleton ☎ 928 84 25 25 🕐 Lunch, dinner

Punta Fariones (££)
In a neat blue and white building at the heart of the village beside the little harbour, this modest café-restaurant serves good fresh fish and seafood at reasonable prices.
✉ Calle La Quemadita ☎ 928 84 25 58 🕐 All day

PARQUE NACIONAL DE TIMANFAYA

El Diablo (££)
This broad, low, circular building is situated beside Timanfaya's hottest hot spot. The first of Manrique's landscape architectural works, it has panoramic views, and very enjoyable traditional Canarian cuisine cooked over heat rising directly from the earth.
✉ Islote de Hilario, Parque Nacional de Timanfaya ☎ 928 84 00 57 🕐 Lunch

PLAYA BLANCA

El Almacén de la Sal (£££)

On the waterfront in a converted salt store, this elegant, characterful place has a cool, attractive stone and timber interior. The menu offers the best of fresh fish and meat dishes, and many local specialities. Some live music.

✉ 12 Paseo Marítimo ☎ 928 51 78 85 🕐 Lunch, dinner (snacks all day). Closed Tue

Brisa Marina (££)

Half-way along the waterside walkway of the old part of the village, this popular place concentrates on tasty fresh fish and seafood.

✉ 10 Playa Blanca ☎ 928 51 71 53 🕐 Lunch

La Cocina del Mar (££)

Lovely waterside tables at this beautifully positioned restaurant near the harbour end of Playa Blanca's attractive promenade. A talkative mynah bird entertains.

✉ 3 Avenida de las Playas ☎ 928 51 19 33 🕐 All day

PUERTO DEL CARMEN

El Ancla (££)

Polished wood, quarry tile floors and a position beside the harbour add to the charm of this deservedly popular restaurant. Sample Canary cheeses, choose grilled fresh fish and finish with orange and honey dessert.

✉ 12 C/Nuestra Señora del Carmen 🕐 Lunch, dinner

La Cañada (£)

Unassuming restaurant just off Avenida de las Mayas, serving up delicious local dishes.

✉ Calle de César Manrique 3 ☎ 928 51 19 33 🕐 Lunch, dinner

Cristóbal Colón (£££)

Elegant, tasteful, with impeccable service, and ornate tiles and pictures. Food is mainly French-style, ranging from fresh fish to the seven-course menu gastronomique. Extensive wine list.

✉ 47 Centro Commercial, Matagorda ☎ 928 51 25 54 🕐 Lunch, dinner

Especiero (££)

This enjoyable, good-quality, air-conditioned restaurant with spectacular sea views is a real find. Try one of the speciality flambé dishes, or select from an excellent and very reasonably priced menu.

✉ 42 Avenida de las Playas ☎ 928 51 21 82 🕐 Lunch, dinner

La Fontaine (££)

A fine selection of ambitious fish and meat dishes with emphasis on the local. It is advisable to make a reservation.

✉ 9 Calle Teide ☎ 928 51 42 51 🕐 Dinner. Closed Tue

Lani's Bistro (££)

The Lani group run seven differently styled restaurants along the Avenida. Enjoy an international range of dishes, desserts and pastries.

✉ 24 Avenida de las Playas ☎ 928 51 23 02 🕐 10AM–midnight

EATING OUT IN PUERTO DEL CARMEN

There are said to be over 200 restaurants in town, mostly along the Avenida de las Playas. They range from pizzerias to balti to Tex-Mex. Few have any local specialities – Spanish dishes are likely to be gazpacho, paella and other mainland favourites. Restaurants often display photos of the dishes as well as a menu in four or five languages. Few restaurants accept reservations, so stroll along the avenue and choose one which takes your fancy.

67

TAPAS TWO

Although *tapas* should not be expensive it's as well to check the price in advance or as you are going along. It's quite easy to spend more on a successsion of snacks than you would on a proper meal. Note too that some kinds of *jamon serrano* are very expensive. Locals sometimes display a curious litter-lout habit of throwing toothpicks, serviettes, sometimes even bits of prawn shell straight onto the floor by the bar. Unless you are a local don't copy them!

Lani's Grill (££)
Good cooking and quick, polite service in several languages. With a rustic wood and ceramic interior, the Grill offers a wide range of meat and fish dishes.
⊠ **Avenida de las Playas**
☎ **928 51 34 07**
🕓 **6PM–midnight**

Lani's Ristorante Italiano (££)
Tiled floors, lots of leafy ferns, purple tablecloths and a little bit of mock Roman décor make this a pleasant setting for good, authentic Italian cooking. Tasty hot rolls are served with garlic butter, and a complimentary liqueur is given after the meal.
⊠ **29 Avenida de las Playas**
☎ **928 51 34 07** 🕓 **12–12**

La Lonja del Fondeadero (£–££)
In the heart of the old port, this traditional boisterous quayside fried-fish bar has plain wooden tables around a central bar, tiled walls and excellent fish dishes at low prices, including paella.
⊠ **Calle Varadero** ☎ **928 51 13 77** 🕓 **All day**

O Bota Fumeiro (££)
An excellent seafood restaurant on Playa de los Pocillos, near San Antonio hotel.
⊠ **Centro Commercial Costa Luz, Avenida de las Playas**
🕓 **Lunch, dinner**

La Ola (£££)
Cool elegance and blue and white décor reflect a magical setting by the sea.

Impeccable service and wonderful views. Start with *papas arrugadas*, choose from a traditional fish or meat main course, and finish with good ice-cream or cakes.
⊠ **10 Avenida de las Playas**
☎ **928 51 42 28** 🕓 **12–12**

O'Orreo (££)
Highly professional cooking, attentive service and the Jameos Playa location makes this one of the best beachside eateries, with excellent, good-value meat, fish and pasta dishes. Inexpensive children's dishes. Good
⊠ **Centro Commercial Jameos L66** ☎ **928 51 18 52** 🕓 **All day**

Terraza Playa (££)
Steps decorated with black and white pebbles lead down to a beachside terrace under palm trees. This is a lovely spot, with good food and service, all at a reasonable price.
⊠ **28 Avenida de las Playas**
☎ **928 51 54 17** 🕓 **Lunch, dinner**

El Varadero (££)
Fishing boats pull up alongside this former warehouse, which serves good *tapas*, fresh fish and traditional *papas arrugadas*.
⊠ **34 Calle Varadero**
☎ **928 51 31 62** 🕓 **Lunch, dinner**

LA SANTA

Los Charcones (£)
On the main road skirting the village a couple of kilometres from the sports

resort, this unpretentious restaurant has a strongly Spanish feel and specialises in locally caught fish and seafood.

✉ On Tinajo road
☎ 928 84 03 27 ⏰ Lunch, dinner

La Santa (££)
Popular non-Spanish meat dishes like stroganoff, pepper steak, or *escalope Milanese* dominate a menu geared mainly towards the residents of nearby La Santa Sport.

✉ On Tinajo road ☎ 928 84 03 53 ⏰ Lunch, dinner

Verde Mar (£)
Encounter the Lanzaroteños on their home ground and get a taste of the fried dishes they love at this basic bar in the village square.

✉ Plaza Iglesia ☎ 928 84 00 19 ⏰ All day

TEGUISE

Acatife (££)
Ambitious and delicious cooking such as cucumber soup with smoked salmon, rabbit in red wine, charcoal-grilled meat, and Lanzarote wines, served in a wonderfuly restored historic building.

✉ 4 Calle San Miguel
☎ 928 84 50 37 ⏰ Lunch, dinner. Closed Sun and Mon

La Galeria (££)
Relaxed, characterful place serving *tapas*, a range of fish dishes, stews and desserts, with live music on occasions.

✉ 8 Calle Nueva
☎ 928 84 50 44
⏰ Lunch, dinner. Closed Sat

UGA

Casa Gregorio (££)
A traditional Lanzarote inn serving the Island's speciality dishes, including fried kid. On Sundays a traditional rich *puchero* stew is served.

✉ Uga 48 ☎ 928 83 01 08 ⏰ Lunch. Closed Tue

YAIZA

El Campo (££)
Overshadowed by La Era's reputation, this is another good eating place in this lovely village, serving local and international dishes.

✉ By the football ground
☎ 928 83 03 44 ⏰ 9–11

La Era (££)
Excellent cooking of local specialities and a good value set meal are on offer here, in an agreeable old–fashioned atmosphere and delightful setting. The restaurant consists of a series of small rooms and tables laid with homespun gingham. The cool white Malvasia wines are made on the farm's vineyard.

✉ Carretera General ☎ 928 83 00 16 ⏰ Lunch, dinner

YÉ

El Volcan (££)
This big, cheerful country-style restaurant is situated on the edge of Yé village in the hills near Mirador del Rio. Try the great mixed starter of *gofio*, figs, dried fish, sweet potatoes and goat's cheese.

✉ Plaza de los Remedios
☎ 928 83 01 56 ⏰ 10–7. Closed Sun

WORTH A SPECIAL JOURNEY

La Era is not just a restaurant, and is worth visiting. Part of a fascinating complex of 300-year-old farm buildings and outbuildings, La Era is one of just three Yaiza buildings pre-dating the 18th-century volcanic eruptions. It was beautifully restored under César Manrique's direction. A pretty little traditional green-framed gateway leads into a quiet courtyard, off which a bar, a shop and a garden form part of the same complex.

69

Fuerteventura

WIND FROM AFRICA

The Sahara sands that cover large areas of Fuerteventura have taken some time to arrive. Although windy on the island, most of the time the air is clear and comes from the north. However, when the sirocco blows, the dry wind from the east, it brings dust as well as heat. The 'dust' is in fact tiny particles of sand. The sirocco blows for short spells at a time, and mainly in winter.

AJUY

Casa Pepín (££)
At this fishing harbour on the west coast, a short drive from Pájara, enjoy local dishes, including kid meat, fish and seafood.
✉ Calle Puerto Azul 4 ☎ 928 16 15 29 🕐 Wed–Sun 10–10, Mon & Tue 10–5

ANTIGUA

El Molino de Antigua (££)
A grain store beside the restored 200-year-old windmill just outside Antigua has been turned into a rustic-style restaurant, offering tasty local dishes in a tranquil setting.
✉ El Molino, Carretera de Antigua s/n, km 20 ☎ 928 87 84 82 🕐 Lunch, dinner. Closed Sun

BETANCURÍA

Casa de Santa Maria (££–£££)
Opposite the much visited church of Santa Maria, so something of a tourist trap, but still managing to serve enjoyable local food in an atmospheric former 16th–century farmhouse.
✉ Plaza de la Concepcion ☎ 928 87 82 82

CALETA DE FUSTES

Mona Lisa (££)
Good, varied menu of national and international dishes, huge pizzas and salads, and friendly, efficient service. A great place to take the children.
✉ Urb. Puerto Caleta ☎ 928 16 32 07 🕐 Lunch, dinner

CORRALEJO

Café Latin (£)
A waterfront café with a choice of simple meals at tables actually on the water's edge.
✉ 21 Avenida Marítima 🕐 All day

La Chama (£)
Excellent value fresh fish, grills, *tapas* and noisy locals kicking up a good atmosphere in which to enjoy a pleasant meal.
✉ opposite Banco Santander ☎ no phone 🕐 Lunch, dinner

El Corsario (££)
Spanish music rings out of this lively bar-restaurant. There's wood panelling inside, and a wood-covered street terrace with outdoor tables. Local dishes include a starter of Manchego cheese, *churros de pescado* (fried fish), and there are also foreign dishes like fillet steak with pepper sauce. Fresh-fish dishes are priced by weight.
✉ 12 Calle La Iglesia
☎ 928 86 71 65
🕐 Lunch, dinner

Country Kitchen (££)
Traditional British food is on offer here, including fish and chips, steak and kidney pie, chilli con carne or chicken curry. Finish off with apple crumble. Portions are generous.
✉ 50 Calle Isaac Peral
☎ 928 53 56 42 🕐 Lunch, dinner

Fogelera (£)
Eat indoors or at tables on a beachside walkway with

a view towards Lobos island, at this budget bar-restaurant with a Spanish feel.

🖂 **End of Avenida Maritima**
🕓 Lunch, dinner

La Marquesina (££)

It is pleasant to sit at the outdoor tables of this relaxed waterside bar-restaurant close to the small jetty where boats pull up. Fresh fish a speciality.

🖂 **Calle El Muelle Chico**
☎ 928 86 75 22 🕓 **All day**

Il Mulino (££)

Authentic Italian cooking under a wooden arcade in a tiled alley by the harbour. Numerous meat and non-meat sauces to accompany fresh home-made pasta.

🖂 **Calle García Escámez**
☎ **928 86 71 05**
🕓 Lunch, dinner

El Rincon de Perico (££)

Excellent *tapas* and half-portions as well as complete meals from a very authentic range of local dishes like *sancocho*, *gofio escaldo*, *potaje de berros*, *papas arrugadas*, and more.

🖂 **40 Calle Gen Linares**
☎ **928 53 57 22**
🕓 **All day**

El Sombrero (££)

Mock-rustic décor and a touch of style distinguish this good Mexican restaurant right on the harbour front. Sit indoors or outside by the water to enjoy your meal.

🖂 **25 Avenida Marítima**
☎ **928 86 75 31**
🕓 Lunch, dinner

COSTA CALMA

La Taberna (££)

A characterful, relaxing place in little rooms. Latin American and local cuisine, with *pescado a la sal*, fresh fish baked in salt, a popular speciality.

🖂 **Carretera Jandía**
🕓 Lunch, dinner

EL COTILLO

Playa (££)

Go down to the harbour of this small holiday development to enjoy the fresh fish and shellfish catch of the day.

🖂 **El Cotillo harbour**
🕓 Lunch, dinner

PLAYA JANDÍA

Saavedra (££)

Go downstairs in the commercial centre to find Spanish atmosphere and Spanish food.

🖂 **4 Plaza Cirillo Lopez, Jandía** 🕓 Lunch, dinner

PUERTO DEL ROSARIO

La Marquesina (££)

A popular spot to enjoy the day's fresh fish and seafood dishes.

🖂 **6 Calle Pizarro** ☎ **928 53 00 30** 🕓 Lunch, dinner

Antiguo (£££)

One of the island's best restaurants, the Antiguo offers a reliable menu of good, well-prepared food with Spanish and international flavours.

🖂 **Hotel Fuerteventura, 45 Playa Blanca** ☎ **928 85 11 50**
🕓 Lunch, dinner

LOCAL INFORMATION

On Fuerteventura pick up a free copy of the small monthly listings magazine Grapevine, which has some useful resort maps, marked with places to eat, drink and be merry. There are also bus and ferry timetables and general information.

Lanzarote

PRICES

For a double room, per night in the period Jan–Mar, booked independently, expect to pay:
£ = under 60 euros
££ = 60–120 euros
£££ = over 120 euros

RUN FOR IT

Although Club La Santa facilities can only be used by the sport resort's residents, outsiders may enter for the major international prize events held at, or organised by Club La Santa, such as the Volcano Triathlon (1.5km swim, 40km cycle plus 10km run) or the Ironman Triathlon (3.8km swim, 180km cycle plus 42km run). Prizes can amount to £30,000 or more.

Tour operators featuring Lanzarote offer a wide range of high-quality villas with pools, and less expensive self-catering holiday apartments, as well as the small number of hotels listed here.

ARRECIFE

Lancelot (££)
Cool and comfortable, this medium-sized, medium-priced hotel has a strong Spanish feel. It faces sandy Playa del Reducto beach.
✉ **9 Avenida Mancomunidad**
☎ **928 80 50 99**

COSTA TEGUISE

Beatriz (££)
This hotel is some distance from the sea and the resort's centre. Black, white and red marble in the cool, spacious public areas reflects Lanzarote's colours. Amazing atria have waterfalls, a stream, lush greenery. Outside, a large swimming area has several pools.
✉ **3 Calle Atalaya**
☎ **928 59 15 13**

Gran Meliá Salinas (£££)
Very stylish, with superb cactus gardens in front, this luxurious Las Cucharas beachfront hotel encircles wonderful watery tropical gardens inside. Rooms are of the highest standard, with beautiful bathrooms and sea views. Top-quality restaurant.
✉ **Avenida Islas Canarias**
☎ **928 59 00 40**

Teguise Playa (££)
Hanging gardens and vast public areas with decorative pools welcome you into an extremely well-equipped comfortable modern hotel, well-placed in the Jablillo area of the resort.
✉ **Avenida del Jablillo**
☎ **928 59 06 54**

Los Zocos Resort (££)
Self-cater or eat in the pleasant buffet restaurant at this popular family holiday complex not far from the beach. There's a safe, attractive pool area, landscaped grounds and plenty of amusements for all age groups.
✉ **Avenida Islas Canarias**
☎ **928 59 21 22**

PLAYA BLANCA

Lanzarote Princess (££)
This attractive, comfortably equipped hotel, arranged around an impressive swimming pool area, is set back from the sea. It has beautiful interiors of marble, greenery and water.
✉ **Playa Blanca (near Playa Dorada)** ☎ **928 51 71 08**

Timanfaya Palace (££)
The spectacular white exterior of domes, turrets, timbers and openings is modelled on traditional local architecture, while a curved frontage à la Manrique arches towards the sea. The lavish interiors are cool, comfortable and stylish. The hotel has a narrow but pleasant sandy beach in front, lined by a walkway.
✉ **Playa Blanca (Limones end)** ☎ **928 51 76 76**

PUERTO DEL CARMEN

Beatriz Playa (££)
Adjacent to the beachfront promenade, this comfortable, popular and family-friendly hotel with attractive poolside gardens and terraces is a few paces from Matagorda's shops and restaurants. There is periodic noise from aircraft – the airport runway lies behind the hotel – but none at night.

✉ **Matagorda**
☎ **928 59 08 28**

Los Fariones (££)
One of the island's older hotels, the Fariones stands between the old harbour and the long sandy main beach. A civilised tranquillity pervades the hotel, and the pool area and shaded waterside terraces are delightful.

✉ **Puerto del Carmen**
☎ **928 51 01 75**

Los Jameos Playa (£££)
An impressive, luxurious hotel in the style of a grand Canarian mansion. Wooden galleries surround a delightful central patio. The extensive palm-shaded outdoor terrace has swimming pools and an excellent restaurant.

✉ **Playa de los Pocillos**
☎ **928 51 17 17**

La Perla (£)
A simple, well-kept little hotel at the end of the beach and close to the old port; the bright rooms are equipped with private balconies.

✉ **7 Avenida de la Playas**
☎ **928 51 44 14**

Riu Palace Lanzarote (££)
Hardly visible from the road, this elegant, comfortable low-rise hotel is set back from Playa de los Pocillos. Greenery, glass, marble and cacti give a cool, stylish air.

✉ **6 Calle Suiza**
☎ **920 51 24 14**

San Antonio (££)
One of the original hotels on the island, the San Antonio stands in a quiet part of the resort, between Playa de los Pocillos and the main beach. Pleasant palm and cactus gardens, heated outdoor pool.

✉ **84 Avenida de las Playas**
☎ **928 51 42 00**

LA SANTA

Club La Santa (££).
This is one of the most highly rated sports resorts in the world. The range of facilities and programme of sports and sightseeing activities is tremendous and reserved exclusively for guests staying at the resort. There are several swimming pools, seven restaurants, a late-night disco and extensive facilities for young children.

✉ **Club La Santa, Tinajo**
☎ **928 59 99 95 (0161 790 9890)**

YAIZA

Finca de las Salinas (££)
Plenty of charm. It's cool and peaceful inside, with flagstone floors and a lounge with cane seats arranged around palm trees growing through an open 'ceiling'.

✉ **17 Calle La Cuesta**
☎ **928 83 03 25**

THE MANRIQUE EFFECT

Lanzarote lacks the high-rise hotels of other popular Canary Islands. César Manrique decided on a maximum five floors for hotels in a Zona Turística (Tourist Zone). Even here, he laid down design guidelines which have been broadly followed. The result is a great success: a seafront not dominated by cheap concrete skyscrapers, but instead with unostentatious white buildings on a human scale, which retain a certain link with the island culture.

Fuerteventura

BOOK A BARGAIN

Most of the hotels listed are available as part of package holidays from tour operators, including return charter flights to the island. Some of the hotels can only be booked through travel agencies, and some only take half-board guests. If you're travelling independently, you'll usually pay more than package tourists – unless you're prepared to make a last-minute call direct to the hotels. Then, any vacant rooms will often be available at low prices.

On Fuerteventura the emphasis is on small-to-medium sized, modern, budget complexes of self-contained chalet-style family accommodation which combine self-catering apartments or chalets with a central reception area and some hotel amenities such as pools, play areas and restaurants.

CALETA DE FUSTES

Caleta Amarilla Aparthotel (£)
About 1½km out of town, this plain and simple budget holiday apartment complex (actually two, separated by a road) offers chalet-style rooms with balcony or terrace, kitchenette, and all meals and drinks pre-paid on an 'all inclusive' basis.
✉ **Caleta de Fustes, Antigua**
☎ **928 16 31 25**

Castillo Beach Bungalows Sol (£)
The simple chalet-style self-catering bungalows at this popular complex are spread through a site with plenty of enjoyable facilities for family holidays, including several pools with waterside bars, play areas, tennis courts and other games. The drawbacks are that there is overhead noise from the nearby airport, and it's 2km to the beach – but you can get there on a little shuttle train.
✉ **Caleta de Fustes, Antigua**
☎ **928 16 30 01**

Club El Castillo (£)
One of many low-rise, inexpensive aparthotel complexes, this member of the Barceló group offers accommodation in one- or two-storey simple beachside bungalows. Room facilities are limited but the reception area and public facilities include restaurants, bars, a disco, TV room, games room, swimming pools and a childrens' play park, as well as a handy shop for self-catering guests.
✉ **Caleta de Fustes, Antigua**
☎ **928 16 31 00**

Las Villas del Castillo (£)
This unusual, agreeable complex has 122 self-contained villas in a garden setting with palms and greenery, close to the beach. Each villa is effectively a hotel room with its own kitchenette and terrace, though there are no phones or TVs. The complex has its own attractive pool and sunbathing area.
✉ **Caleta de Fustes, Antigua**
☎ **928 16 30 44**

CORRALEJO

Los Delfines (£)
This simple, white two-storey complex of small self-catering apartments, each with its own little balcony or terrace, is attractively arranged around a pool area. The complex has a TV room, on-site supermarket, and some leisure facilities, such as squash courts. There's also a buffet restaurant, giving the option to eat out if preferred. Situated on the edge of Corralejo, some 200m from the beach.
✉ **Corralejo** ☎ **928 53 51 53**

Lobos Bahai Aparthotel (££)

An attractive pool and agreeable poolside bar are at the heart of this better-than-average complex of plain white two-storey buildings. All rooms have a kitchen area, balcony or terrace, and facilities include bars, restaurants, evening shows, TV room, games rooms, gym, and more, as well as a little supermarket for self-catering.

✉ **Corralejo** ☎ **928 86 71 43**

Riu Oliva Beach (££)

A comfortable, well-placed family hotel with small rooms but good access to the vast, beautiful beach, a swimming and sunbathing area, and an all day children's club. Self-cater or choose half-board.

✉ **Playas de Corralejo (south of town)** ☎ **928 86 61 00**

Riu Palace Tres Islas (£££)

Standing right on the immense beach that edges the dunes, this stylish, comfortable and well-equipped 365-roomed hotel is ideally placed for exploring the north of the island. Luxurious bedrooms have dark wood furnishings and private terraces looking over either sea or dunes. Palms and lawns surround a lovely swimming and sunbathing area.

✉ **Playas de Corralejo (south of town)** ☎ **928 53 57 00**

JANDÍA

Los Gorriones Sol (££)

Beautiful, isolated position right on Sotavento beach with pools, sun terraces and gardens. Windsurfing school based at the hotel.

✉ **North of Jandía resort** ☎ **928 54 70 25**

Iberostar Palace (£££)

This large, well-equipped 4-star complex has comfortable accommodation and an abundance of facilities for almost 900 guests.

✉ **Urbanización Las Gaviotas** ☎ **928 54 04 44**

Mar Sol Apartments (££)

Dark hills and golden beach provide the setting for this pleasant apartment complex with its own pools, restaurant, sports facilities and play areas. There's nightly entertainment and a disco, with more entertainment and facilities in the centre of the resort, about 10 minutes' walk away.

✉ **Morro Jable, Jandía** ☎ **928 54 13 25**

PUERTO DEL ROSARIO

Hotel Fuerteventura (£££)

This stylish former *parador* (state-run hotel) achieves a high standard of simple, polished elegance and comfort. A rather unappealing barrack-like exterior is mitigated by attractive greenery. A less than ideal location between the airport and the capital town is likewise partly offset by the seashore setting. It has 50 rooms, a swimming pool and tennis courts, the bar and a good restaurant are open to the public.

✉ **Playa Blanca** ☎ **928 85 11 50**

Markets & Souvenirs

AFRICAN TRADERS

Colourfully dressed Africans in the market squares of Lanzarote and Fuerteventura bring an exotic note to the Spanish scene. These West African trading families, often Senegalese, make the boat trip specifically to sell in European markets, and stay for several months. Usually the whole family sits at different stalls selling very similar goods, or women may sit together grooming each other, breast-feeding, while older children tap idly at African drums.

CRAFTS

Most typical of the island crafts are fine weaving, embroidery and lacework, seen in high-quality tablecloths, placemats, bed-spreads and handkerchiefs. You'll also see good costume jewellery (often including *peridot*, the translucent semi-precious volcanic stone), basketware, straw hats, and unusual local pottery, traditionally made without a potters' wheel. Delicate woodwork includes *timples*, the tiny Canarian stringed instrument that originated in Teguise.

Almost every town has its weekly or even daily market. These rarely have any of the fruit, vegetables or live chickens of traditional country markets elsewhere. Stallholders are usually Africans selling African handmade goods; northern Europeans selling their own craftwork; and Spanish market traders selling either linens, embroidery, lace and other cloth goods, or ceramics.

African Craftwork

Items for sale will include carved wooden masks, wooden toys, studded or tooled leatherwork and authentic African drums. In addition there are historic tribal artefacts, such as ancient ceremonial masks, which should perhaps not have found their way into the market. Nothing has a marked price. Don't buy ivory goods (illegal in the European Union) or cheap European and Far Eastern imitations.

Local Lace, Crochet and Embroidery

The most common items are tablecloths, placemats, napkins, bedlinen and handkerchiefs. These are by no means always cheap, but are good value for such high-quality handmade work, and have distinctively Spanish designs and character.

Ceramics

Tiles, glazed pottery and attractively handpainted crockery make excellent gifts or souvenirs but can be heavy and fragile for air-travellers. However, small items, well-packed, make a distinctive and worthwhile purchase.

Souvenirs

Other attractive souvenirs of Lanzarote and Fuerteventura include basketwork, a local semi-precious stone called *olivina*, local silverwork and César Manrique T-shirts.

Teguise

The main shopping event for many visitors is the Sunday market in Teguise, which operates from 9AM to 2PM, and is one of the Canaries' largest. A vast array of stalls, surrounded by shoppers, is crammed into almost every inch of the little town, until Teguise is bursting with the crowd. The carnival-like atmosphere is often enhanced by colourful folklore shows and traditional events.

Other markets
Arrecife

Saturday morning at El Charco de San Ginés

Costa Teguise

Friday afternoon in Plaza Pueblo Marinero

Mancha Blanca

During the Mancha Blanca fiesta in September there is a big street market of traders selling their wares from all of the Canary Islands.

Duty Free Shopping

DUTY FREE SHOPPING

Tha Canary Islands have a long history as a duty-free zone. Even though – as part of Spain – they are now subject to EU law, the islands continue to have exemption from certain taxes and duties on goods imported from outside the EU. In the main towns, especially tourist resorts, dozens of shops offer electronic goods, cameras, binoculars and other optical equipment, CD and DVD players, perfumes and other luxury items at discount prices.

Alcohol of all types is generally good value. Beware though – do not simply assume that 'duty-free' prices are a bargain: many tourists discover too late that they have paid almost as much (and sometimes more) than the usual shop price. Most of the shopkeepers are Indian, not Spanish, and are accustomed to haggling over prices. Be especially on your guard against fakes and imitations, counterfeit or defective items, and watches or similar goods with fake designer names. Remember the bona fide electronic goods should be accompanied by proper international warranties and service details.

Lanzarote

Bazar Karina
✉ Avenida de las Playas (near Hotel San Antonio), Puerto del Carmen

Bazar TPV
✉ Avenida de las Playas (harbour end), Puerto del Carmen

Pedro y Nicholás Martín
✉ 2 Calle Gen Goded, Arrecife

Perfumeria Maja
Top perfumes, as well as fine lace and cotton, at discount prices.
✉ Avenida de las Playas (near Fariones Hotel), Puerto del Carmen

RT Electronics
Cameras and watches at low prices.
✉ CC Jameos Playa, Playa de los Pocillos

Swiss Heritage
This bright, smart shop sells gold and diamond jewellery at tax-free prices.
✉ CC Jameos Playa, Playa de los Pocillos
☎ 928 51 56 02

Fuerteventura

Bazar Insular
✉ Calle Gen Franco, Corralejo

Bazar Korina
✉ Calle Gen Franco, Corralejo

MANRIQUE DESIGNS

Fundacíon César Manrique Shops
T-shirts and other clothes with Manrique logos and designs, jewellery and other goods to his design, and prints of his work.
✉ Main shop: Taro de Tahíche. Other shops: 26 José Betancort, Arrecife; 10 Diaz Otilía, Arrecife, La Lonja, Teguise; Avenida de las Playas, Puerto del Carmen

FLOWERS THAT FLY

Exotic, Canary-grown *strelitzias* – bird-of-paradise flowers – are widely available and make a popular, impressive gift. They should be ordered in good time, picked up on the day of your departure, and are specially wrapped and packaged for air travel. Alternatively, they can be bought in the departure lounge at Arrecife airport.

EDIBLE SOUVENIRS

Consumables that make interesting presents or tasty reminders of your stay include *mojo* sauces, available in small gift packs, and local wine, which can be chosen and sampled in the bodegas of Lanzarote's Geria Valley (► 26).

Sport – on Water

WIND (FOR WINDSURFERS)

It is the regular, strong north-by-northwest trade wind (known as Los Alisios and often reaching force 4 or 5) blowing in from the Atlantic that makes Lanzarote and Fuerteventura such an excellent centre for wind-surfing. The winds don't always blow, however: the average reliability rate is around 50 per cent in winter and 60–75 per cent in summer. The western, windward coasts can offer thrilling sport for experienced windsurfers, but beware – El Cotillo beach on Fuerteventura is said to break more kit than any other surf location in Europe!

BIG GAME FISHING

Hunting for shark, barracuda, swordfish, marlin, tuna, wahoo, dorado and the other big Atlantic fish is popular. Hire a boat or join an excursion.

Lanzarote

PUERTO CALERO

Catlanza
Daily deep sea fishing excursions by catamaran. Yachts and motorboats for private hire.
✉ Puerto Calero ☎ 928 51 30 22

Fuerteventura

CORRAJELO

Barvik
Hunting for shark, marlin, tuna, wahoo, dorado and other big Atlantic fish.
✉ Muelle Deportivo ☎ 928 17 51 55

Pez Velero
Daily excursions in 33ft catamaran fishing for barracuda, tuna, bluefish and bass.
✉ Muelle Deportivo ☎ 928 86 61 73

DIVING & SCUBA DIVING

Good underwater visibility, in a climate zone where diving is possible year round, has made this a favourite sport on the two islands. The underwater lava has created many reefs, caves and unusual rock formations. There is an abundance of wildlife to be seen, including sharks, eels, octopus and rays, as well as big fish, sponges, anenomes, crustaceans and colourful coral.

Lanzarote

COSTA TEGUISE

Calipso Diving
International courses in diving and scuba diving.
✉ Centro Commercial Nautical, Avenida de los Islas Canarias ☎ 928 59 08 79

Diving Lanzarote
High-quality scuba diving centre with variety of hire and excursion options, including night diving.
✉ 104 Apartado de Correos, Costa Teguise ☎ 928 59 04 07

PUERTO DEL CARMEN

Atlantic Diving Center
Diving courses from the main beach.
✉ Aparthotel Fariones Playa, 2 Calle Acatife ☎ 928 51 02 00

RC Diving
Try-out lessons, training courses, organised dives. Prices include equipment.
✉ 38 Avenida de las Playas ☎ 928 00 34 28

Safari Diving
This PADI five-star, highly professional centre for diving welcomes divers of all qualifications, as well as disabled divers, beginners, non-divers, and children, for a wide range of courses lasting from 4 hours to 21 days. Organised dives include night diving. Prices include all equipment.
✉ Playa Chica (near the port) ☎ 928 51 04 96

Fuerteventura

CORRALEJO

Dive Center Corralejo
Enjoy a whole day's dive with instructor, including audio-visual training. If you are an experienced diver with certification and logbook, the Dive Center offers boat dives daily (except Sun) from 8:30AM–1:30PM.
✉ **29 Apartado de Correos**
☎ **928 86 62 43**

SURFING
Fantastic wind and waves make these islands great for surfers.

Lanzarote

LA SANTA

La Santa Surf
This is *not* part of La Santa Sport complex. Take a surfing safari – this includes transport, lunch, equipment hire and instruction. Equipment rental only also possible.
✉ **La Santa** ☎ **928 84 02 79**

Fuerteventura

CORRALEJO

Ineika Funcenter Surfschool
A range of courses from one to 14 days, fully inclusive of equipment, transfers and video training.
✉ **53 Ineika Apts** ☎ **928 53 57 44**

Natural Surf
Instruction courses and equipment hire.
✉ **Calle Palangre** ☎ **928 86 73 07**

Ventura Surf
Instruction courses and equipment hire
✉ **Maya de la Galera** ☎ **928 86 62 95**

WINDSURFING
This is by far the most popular sport in the Canary Islands. Every main resort has facilities for rentals and instruction. Fuerteventura is considered one of the world's best locations for windsurfing, and Jandía's Playa de Sotavento is the site of the annual World Windsurfing Championships mid-July to mid-August.

Lanzarote

COSTA TEGUISE

Surf Club Celeste
Courses and equipment hire by the hour or day.
✉ **Centro Commercial las Maretas** ☎ **928 59 08 79**

Fuerteventura

CORRALEJO

Flag Beach Windsurf Center
✉ **Grandes Playas** ☎ **928 53 55 39**

Ventura Surf
Tuition and rentals from one hour to 14 days.
✉ **8 Hoplaco Aptos** ☎ **928 86 62 95**

PLAYA BARCA

Center René Egli
The Jandía peninsula's principal windsurfing base, with tuition and rentals, right on Sotavento beach.
✉ **Sol Hotel Los Gorriones** ☎ **928 54 74 83**

WIND (FOR HOLIDAYMAKERS)

The north-by-northwest trade wind brings stable, rain-free days with some cloud. On the north or west of the islands, the wind can be troublesome, and the cloud cover excessive. In the south and east, it means perfect holiday weather. The occasional alternatives are the moist southerly winds or the unpleasant, warm dry sirocco that blows sand over from the Sahara.

Sport – on Land

GRIN AND BARE IT

Topless sunbathing is acceptable on all beaches, especially the main beaches of Puerto del Carmen, Costa Teguise, Playa Blanca, Corralejo and Jandía. Naturism, or stripping off completely, is not acceptable on resort beaches, but common on any secluded stretch of coast, or beaches outside resorts, such as Playa Papagayo on Lanzarote, or, on Fuerteventura, the Corralejo beach away from the hotels.

AERIAL SPORTS

Lanzarote

Aviador Flying School
Excursions and lessons, based at the airport.
☎ 928 35 41 93

Lanzarote Skydive Centre
Parachute jumps.
☎ 928 84 01 14

CYCLING

Thanks to the dry weather and lack of traffic, cycle touring is fun on these islands. Choose between easy-going flatter terrain near the resorts, and more challenging hills in the interior.

Lanzarote

COSTA TEGUISE

Hot Bike
Bike hire by week, day or half-day; maps, baby seats and the like are also available. The company also organises bike-and-jeep outings.
✉ Near Playa de las Cucharas ☎ 928 59 03 04

Tommy's Bikes
This friendly company gives free advice and maps, and organises excursions and tours. A typical excursion lasts a whole day.
✉ 14 Apartado de Correos, Calle de la Galeta, Galeon Playa (near Playa del Jablillo)
☎ 928 59 23 27

Fuerteventura

CORRALEJO

Vulcano Biking
Touring cycles and mountain bikes for hire.
✉ 10 Calle Acorazado España ☎ 928 53 57 06

GOLF

Lanzarote

COSTA TEGUISE

Club de Golf de Costa Teguise
Lanzarote's only golf course is considered one of Europe's most unusual and exciting places to play. The tender green turf of the 18-hole, 72-par course looks dazzling amid the dark hills, cacti and palms. No handicap is required. The course offers a driving range, putting and pitching greens, buggy, trolley and club hire, and a charming club house with bar-restaurant, lounge and pro-shop. Lessons are available.
✉ 2km up Avenida del Golf
☎ 928 59 05 12

HORSE RIDING

Lanzarote

PUERTO DEL CARMEN

Rancho Texas Equestrian Centre
Pony trekking, dressage, jumping and riding lessons available. Also self-catering accommodation for hire.
✉ Signposted from Playa de los Pocillos ☎ 928 17 32 47

UGA

Lanzarote a Caballo
Full- or half-day excursions to the Geria Valley, Playa Quemada or Playa Blanca. Riding lessons also offered.

✉ On Arrecife–Yaiza road, close to Uga ☎ 928 83 03 14

Fuerteventura

CORRALEJO

Fuerteadventure
✉ In the development at Parques Holandés, south of Corralejo

MOTORBIKING
A motorbike is a good way to explore the spectacular terrain. (► panel)

Lanzarote

PUERTO DEL CARMEN

Classic Drive
✉ Avenida de las Playas, Centro Commercial Marítimo
☎ 928 51 23 17

Sunbike & Moto
✉ Centro Commercial Playa Blanca ☎ 928 51 34 40

Fuerteventura

CORRALEJO

Volcano Biking
✉ 10 Calle Acorazado España ☎ 928 53 57 06

SPORTS CENTRES

Lanzarote

COSTA TEGUISE

Toca Sport
Tennis and squash courts are available, plus a swimming pool, gym, sauna, table tennis – and yoga classes.
✉ Avenida del Jablillo
☎ 928 59 06 17

PUERTO DEL CARMEN

Castellana Sport
Fully equipped gym and squash courts open to the public near the beach in Lanzarote's main resort. Offers aerobics classes.
✉ 2 Calle Guanapoy ☎ 928 51 14 93

WALKING
There are numerous possible routes on both islands, but note that walking on the volcanic *malpaís* is difficult and uncomfortable. Don't set off on your own. Take adequate supplies of water, high-energy food and protective gear with you on longer trips.

Lanzarote

TIMANFAYA

Canary Trekking
4km guided volcano walks, one visits a lava tunnel.
☎ 609 537 684
www.canarytrekking.com

ICONA National Parks Walking Service
Two guided walks in Timanfaya National Park, one a volcano walk and one along the coast.
✉ Mancha Blanca Visitor Centre ☎ 928 84 08 39

Fuerteventura

VILLAVERDE

Hannelore von der Twer
Guided walks in many areas including Monte Arena.
✉ Villa Volcana ☎ 928 86 86 90 or 608 92 83 80

MOTORBIKING

The open roads and lack of traffic make the islands attractive places for biking. A few words of warning, however. If you intend going offroad make sure you have a sufficiently powerful machine not to get bogged down in sand, particularly if you have a pillion rider or much luggage. Beware too that lava tracks are extremely bumpy. Fill up with petrol on Saturdays, as on Sundays many petrol stations only have automatic pumps working. The smallest note they accept is 10 euros which will buy far more fuel that you need if you only have a small petrol tank. The free island map from tourist offices usefully shows all petrol stations. And, finally, the cost of hiring a bike may not be any cheaper than a car – shop around as much as you can.

81

Gastronomy & Nightlife

GASTRONOMY

Lanzarote

LA GERIA

Bodegas Barreto
Free wine tasting at this Lanzarote wine cellar.
✉ At El Campesino, on La Geria road ☎ 928 52 07 17
🕐 Daily 10–6:30

MOZAGA

Bodegas Mozaga
Wine tasting and buying at this popular producer of Lanzarote wines.
✉ On Arrecife–Tinajo road
☎ 928 52 04 85 🕐 Daily 8:30AM–6PM

SAN BARTOLOMÉ

El Grifo Bodega and Museo del Vino
The oldest working *bodega* on Lanzarote. Take a look at the old winepress, have a guided stroll in the vineyards and enjoy the wine tasting.
✉ On road to Uga ☎ 928 52 40 12 🕐 Bodega daily 10–4, Museo daily 10:30–6

UGA

El Faro
Tasting of Lanzarote's salty, traditionally made goat's cheeses.
✉ On Teguise–Uga road
☎ 928 17 31 13

CASINOS

PUERTO DEL CARMEN

Casino
Slot machines, blackjack and roulette tables, as well as restaurant, bar and entertainment. Admittance is strictly for over-18s only – and you will most certainly need your passport as proof of age.
✉ 12 Avenida de las Playas
☎ 928 51 50 00 🕐 Slot machines: 11PM–4AM. Bar and game hall: 8PM–4AM. Restaurant: 9PM–2AM

DISCOS AND LATE-NIGHT BARS

All the resorts on both islands have late-night bars with music, but there are few real discos or dance venues. Those listed here open around 9 or 10PM (although they only really start filling up around midnight) and stay open until 2 or 4AM.

Lanzarote

Avenida de las Playas in Puerto del Carmen is Lanzarote's 'entertainment mile', with a large number of late-night bars featuring live music and dancing. The focal point for most of the city's discos and nightclubs is the Centro Atlantico block. Of the other resorts, only Costa Teguise really offers a full choice of bars and discos which are open late.

ARRECIFE

La Antigua
A popular music bar.
✉ 62 Calle José Antonio

La Naos
Five bars and dance floor in a marquee and outdoor terrace; popular with the jet set.
✉ Puerto Naos 🕐 Thu–Sat 11PM–4AM

ARRIETA

Jameos del Agua
After dark on Tuesdays,
Fridays and Saturdays, the
water caverns in the north
of the island become a
popular nightclub, where
crowds drink, dine and
dance in the extraordinary
underground setting. There
is also a folklore show on
these nights.
✉ **Near Arrieta, 26km north
of Arrecife** ☎ **928 84 80 20**
🕐 **Tue, Fri & Sat 7PM–3AM.
Folklore show 11PM**

COSTA TEGUISE

Baobab Club
✉ **2nd floor, Centro Teguise
Playa (Jablillo area)**

PUERTO DEL CARMEN

Basement Club
✉ **Downstairs, Centro
Atlantico**

Dreams Disco
✉ **Downstairs, Centro
Atlantico**

**Harley Rock Diner and
Disco**
The entrance looks like a
juke-box. 'Ladies' Fantasy'
muscle show every
Thursday.
✉ **Upstairs, Centro Columbus**

Moonlight Bay
Bands and cabaret shows
✉ **Playa de los Pocillos**
🕐 **Daily 9PM–4AM**

Papagayo
✉ **Set back from street.
Centro Atlantico**

Paradise
✉ **2nd floor, Centro Columbus**

Fuerteventura

CALETA DE FUSTES

La Polka
✉ **Caleta de Fustes**

CORRALEJO

The Blue Rock
Small bar playing rock and
blues music
✉ **Just off the front, to the
right of the tourist office**

MORRO DEL JABLE

Angels
✉ **Avenida del Saladar**

PUERTO DEL ROSARIO

Taifa
✉ **2 Calle Juan Tadeo
Cabrera**

HOTELS

The main hotels offer
simple entertainment, such
as cabaret, dancing,
karaoke or professional
musicians, every evening
from about 10PM–midnight.
There's no need to be a
guest at the hotel to enjoy
the entertainment.

Melia Salinas Hotel
✉ **Avenida Islas Canarias,
Costa Teguise, Lanzarote**

Timanfaya Palace Hotel
✉ **West of the harbour, Playa
Blanca, Lanzarote**

Los Fariones Hotel
✉ **Harbour end of main
beach, Playa Blanca,
Lanzarote**

Riu Palace Tres Islas
✉ **Playas de Corralejo,
Corralejo, Fuerteventura**

CANARIAN WRESTLING

A favourite spectator sport for
the islanders is their traditional
wrestling (Lucha Canaria), for
which the combatants wear a
particular style of shorts and
shirt. Wrestlers work in teams,
whose members are pitted
against each other one-to-one,
in turns. The fight involves
holding onto the side of your
opponent's shorts and
attempting to throw him to the
ground. It's slow and cautious,
with long waits for sudden
moves. Contests are staged
from time to time, and your
hotel or the tourist office
should have details of
forthcoming matches. This
'clean' sport is very fair and
totally different from
European wrestling. It
provides great family
entertainment. Tourists are
made welcome, and this is a
good way to meet the locals.

LANZAROTE &
FUERTEVENTURA
practical matters

WHAT YOU NEED

● Required ○ Suggested ▲ Not required	UK	Germany	USA	Netherlands	Spain
Passport/National Identity Card	●	●	●	●	●
Visa	▲	▲	▲	▲	▲
Onward or Return Ticket	▲	▲	○	▲	▲
Health Inoculations	▲	▲	▲	▲	▲
Health Insurance	○	○	○	○	○
Travel Insurance	○	○	○	○	○
Driving Licence (national with Spanish translation or International)	○	○	○	○	○
Car Insurance Certificate	●	●	●	●	○
Car Registration Document	●	●	●	●	○

WHEN TO GO

Lanzarote/Fuerteventura

High season

Low season

21°C JAN	21°C FEB	23°C MAR	24°C APR	25°C MAY	26°C JUN	28°C JUL	29°C AUG	29°C SEP	27°C OCT	24°C NOV	21°C DEC

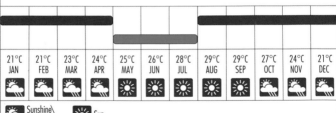

Sunshine\Showers Sun

TIME DIFFERENCES

GMT 12 noon	Canaries 12 noon	Germany 1PM	USA (NY) 7AM	Netherlands 1PM	Spain 1PM

TOURIST OFFICES

In the UK
Spanish National Tourist Office
22–23 Manchester Square
London W1U 3PX
☎ 0207 486 8077
Fax: 0207 486 8034

In the USA
Spanish National Tourist Office
666 Fifth Avenue, 35th floor
New York
NY 10103
☎ 212 265 8822
Fax: 212 265 8864

In Canada
Spanish National Tourist Office
102 Bloor St W, 34th floor
Toronto, Ontario
M4W 3E2
☎ 416 961 3131

ARRIVING

At Lanzarote All flights arrive at Arrecife airport (☎ 928 81 14 50), which lies between Arrecife and its main resort, Puerto del Carmen.
At Fuerteventura All flights arrive at Puerto del Rosario's small airport (☎ 928 85 12 50), which lies between the islands capital and Caleta de Fustes.

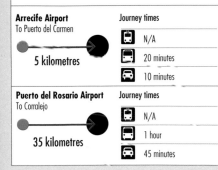

Arrecife Airport
To Puerto del Carmen

5 kilometres

Journey times	
�	N/A
🚌	20 minutes
🚗	10 minutes

Puerto del Rosario Airport
To Corralejo

35 kilometres

Journey times	
🚶	N/A
🚌	1 hour
🚗	45 minutes

MONEY

The euro (€) is the official currency of Spain. Euro banknotes and coins were introduced in January 2002. Banknotes are issued in denominations of 5, 10, 20, 50, 100, 200 and 500 euros; coins in denominations of 1, 2, 5, 10, 20 and 50 cents, and 1 and 2 euros.
Euro traveller's cheques are widely accepted, as are all major credit cards. Credit and debit cards can also be used to withdraw euro notes from ATMs. Spain's former currency, the peseta, went out of circulation in February 2002.

TIME

 Lanzarote and Fuerteventura (and all the Canaries) follow Greenwich Mean Time (GMT), but from late March — when clocks are put forward one hour — until late September, summer time operates (GMT+1).

CUSTOMS

 YES

As the Canaries are a free-trade zone there are no restrictions at all on the amounts of alcohol, tobacco, perfume and other goods that can be brought into the islands. It would be pointless to take most goods into the islands in the expectation of saving money, however: almost everything is cheaper in the Canaries than it is at home. Visitors may bring an unlimited amount of foreign currency but should declare any amount exceeding €6, 000 in cash to avoid difficulties on leaving.

 NO

There are a few obvious exceptions to the above, notably drugs, firearms, obscene material and unlicensed animals.

CONSULATES

UK
☎ 928 26 25 08

Germany
☎ 928 27 57 00

USA
☎ 928 27 12 59

Netherlands
☎ 928 24 23 82

TOURIST OFFICES

Lanzarote

● **Head Office**:
Cabilda Insular de Lanzarote
Consejería de Turismo
Patronato de Turismo
Blas Cabrera Felipe
☎ 928 81 17 62
Fax: 928 80 00 80

Local offices:
● Parque Municipal, Arrecife
☎ 928 81 18 60

● Avenida de las Playas, distinctive beachside hut, Puerto del Carmen
☎ 928 51 53 37

● Ferry harbour, Playa Blanca

Fuerteventura

● **Head office**:
Patronato de Turismo de Fuerteventura
Avenida Constitución 5
Puerto del Rosario
☎ 928 53 08 44
Fax: 928 85 16 95

Local offices:
● Puerto del Rosario airport
☎ 928 86 06 04

● Plaza Pública, Corralejo
☎ 928 86 62 35

● CC Castillo Centro, Caleta de Fustes
☎ 928 16 32 86

● Shopping Centre, Jandía Beach, Morro del Jable
☎ 928 54 07 76

NATIONAL HOLIDAYS

J	F	M	A	M	J	J	A	S	O	N	D
2	1	1(1)	(1)	2	1	1	1		1	1	3

1 Jan	Año Nuevo (New Year's Day)
6 Jan	Los Reyes (Epiphany)
2 Feb	La Candelaria (Candlemas)
19 Mar	San José (St Joseph's Day)
Mar/Apr	Pascua (Easter)
1 May	Día de Trabajo (Labour Day)
May/Jun	Corpus Christi
25 Jul	Santiago (Saint James' Day)
15 Aug	Asunción (Assumption of the Virgin)
12 Oct	Hispanidad (Columbus Day)
1 Nov	Todos los Santos (All Saints' Day)
6 Dec	Constitución (Constitution Day)
8 Dec	Immaculada Concepción (Immaculate Conception)
25 Dec	Navidad (Christmas)

OPENING HOURS

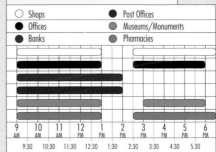

○ Shops	● Post Offices
● Offices	● Museums/Monuments
● Banks	● Pharmacies

9 AM · 10 AM · 11 AM · 12 PM · 1 PM · 2 PM · 3 PM · 4 PM · 5 PM · 6 PM
9:30 · 10:30 · 11:30 · 12:30 · 1:30 · 2:30 · 3:30 · 4:30 · 5:30

In resorts, some shops keep longer hours and may also be open on Sunday. Chemists keep similar hours to other shops but are usually closed on Saturday afternoons. At least one chemist per town is normally open after hours. Many bars open for breakfast around 7AM and stay open till about 1AM or later the following morning. Even outside these hours you can often find a bar open. Expect bars to be closed from 3AM–6AM. Museum opening times can be unpredictable – many open in the mornings only.

ELECTRICITY

The voltage is 220/240v throughout both islands.

Sockets take the standard European two-round-pin plugs. Bring an adaptor for British or American appliances you wish to use with their usual plugs, and Americans should change the voltage setting on appliances.

TIPS/GRATUITIES

Yes ✓ No ✗		
Restaurants (if service not included)	✓	10%
Cafés/bars	✓	change
Tour guides	✓	€ 2
Hairdressers	✓	€ 1–2
Taxis	✓	10%
Chambermaids	✓	€ 1–2
Porters	✓	30–50 cents
Theatre/cinema usherettes	✓	a few cents
Cloakroom attendants	✓	a few cents
Toilets	✓	a few cents

PUBLIC TRANSPORT

Flights
Daily flights between Arrecife (Lanzarote) and Puerto del Rosario (Fuerteventura) take about half an hour and are operated by Iberia and its partners and subsidiary Binter.
Contact Iberia on Lanzarote ☎ 928 84 61 01 and on Fuerteventura ☎ 928 86 05 10.

Buses
Public transport on the islands is mainly confined to a slow rural bus network designed to get villagers to and from the capital (Arrecife in Lanzarote and Puerto del Rosario in Fuerteventura). Buses are always called by their colloquial name, *guaguas* (pronounced 'wahwahs'). Main bus station at Arrecife, Lanzarote: ☎ 928 81 14 56; main bus station at Puerto del Rosario, Fuerteventura: ☎ 928 85 21 66.

Ferries
Between Lanzarote and Fuerteventura (and also to other Canary Islands) ferries are run by:
Transmediterránea (in Arrecife, Lanzarote ☎ 928 81 11 88; in Puerto del Rosario, Fuerteventura ☎ 928 85 08 77)
Betancuria (in Arrecife, Lanzarote ☎ 928 81 25 34; in Corralejo, Fuerteventura ☎ 928 41 72 14)
Fred Olsen (in Playa Blanca, Lanzarote ☎ 928 51 72 66; ticket office also at harbour in Corralejo, Fuerteventura ☎ 928 53 50 90)
Armas (in Playa Blanca, Lanzarote ☎ 928 51 79 12; 90 calle Jose Antonio, Arrecife ☎ 928 82 49 31; the harbour at Corralejo, Fuerteventura ☎ 928 86 70 80).
To Isla de Lobos: Ferry Majorero from Corralejo harbour, Fuerteventura.
To Isla Graciosa: Ferry from Orzola harbour, Lanzarote ☎ 928 84 20 70

CAR RENTAL

Car hire is relatively cheap on Lanzarote, but more expensive on Fuerteventura. Small local firms are efficient, though the (pricier) international firms are also represented. Minor roads on both islands are often little more than dirt tracks and signposting is sporadic.

TAXIS

Cabs have a green 'for hire' light inside the windscreen, and a special SP licence plate ('*servicio público*'). Cabs are inexpensive (dearer on Fuerteventura than Lanzarote, though, simply because distances are longer).

CONCESSIONS

Students Holders of an International Student Identity Card (ISIC) may be able to obtain some concessions on travel, entrance fees etc, but Lanzarote and Fuerteventura are not really geared up for students. There are no youth hostels.

Senior Citizens Lanzarote and Fuerteventura are excellent destinations for older travellers, especially in winter when the resorts are quieter, prices more reasonable and hotels offer very economical long-stay rates. The best deals are available through tour operators who specialise in holidays for senior citizens.

DRIVING

There are no motorways on these two islands.

Speed limit on main roads: **90kph**

Speed limit on urban roads: **60kph** unless indicated

Seatbelts are compulsory for all passengers. Children under 10 (excluding babies in rear-facing baby seats) must ride in the back seats

Driving under the influence of alcohol is strictly illegal, and consequences if involved in an accident will be severe, possibly including a jail term.

Fuel is sold as *Sin plomo* (unleaded) and *Gasoleo* (diesel). Petrol stations are rare on both islands outside the capitals and the main resorts. Most service stations in the interior keep shop hours and don't always take credit cards.

Lanzarote is notorious for accidents. If involved in a serious accident, call the police on 091. If no one is injured, exchange details with other motorists. Hire cars and their drivers should all be insured by the hire company. Hire companies should issue drivers with an emergency number to call in the event of a breakdown.

PHOTOGRAPHY

What to photograph: Volcanic terrain, either as landscapes or in close up, provides extraordinary images. Contrasts of black lava with dazzling white cottages are typical. Also, try immense dunescapes and beaches framed by sky and sea.
Best time to photograph: be aware of the intensity of the light – photographing in the early morning or evening may give the best results.

PERSONAL SAFETY

Crime is not a problem in Lanzarote and Fuerteventura. The greatest risk is theft by another tourist. Put all bags, clothes, etc. in the boot of your car where they cannot be seen. If self-catering, lock all doors and windows before going out.
● Fire is a risk in hotels — locate the nearest fire exit to your room and ensure it is not blocked or locked.
● Do not leave possessions unattended on the beach, beside pools or in cars.
● In an emergency, call the police on 091, otherwise call or visit the Guardia Civil (Arrecife: ☎ 928 81 23 50; Puerto del Rosario: ☎ 928 85 09 09)

Police assistance:
☎ **091**

TELEPHONES

All phone numbers in Spain, including the Canary Islands, have 9 digits, and you must dial the whole number. To use a public payphone, you'll usually need *una tarjeta de teléfono*, a phone card. These are widely available from tobacconists and similar shops. To dial abroad first dial 00, wait for a change of tone, then dial the international code of the country you are calling (see below).

International Dialling Codes

From the Canary Islands (Spain) to:	
UK:	44
Germany:	49
USA:	1
Netherlands:	31
Mainland Spain:	9–digit number only

POST

Post Offices

Post boxes are yellow, and often have a slot marked 'Extranjeros' for mail to foreign countries. Letters or cards to the UK cost 50 cents (up to 20g).
Postcards/letters to the US/Canada cost 75 cents (up to 20g).
Letters within Spain cost 25 cents. Post offices are open Mon–Fri 9–2, Sat 9–1.

HEALTH

Insurance

Nationals of EU and certain other countries can get medical treatment in Spain with the relevant documentation (Form E111 for UK nationals), although private medical insurance is still advised and is essential for all other visitors.

Dental Services

Emergency treatment may be expensive but is covered by most medical insurance (but not by form E111). Keep the bills for insurance claims.

Sun Advice

The sunniest (and hottest) months are July–September with an average of 11 hours sun a day and daytime temperatures of 27–29°C. Particularly during these months you should avoid the midday sun and use a strong sunblock.

Medication

Any essential medicines should be taken with you. Most well-known proprietary brands of analgesics and popular remedies etc are available at all pharmacies. All medicines must be paid for, even if prescribed by a doctor.

Safe Water

Tap water is safe to drink all over the islands, except where signs indicate otherwise. However, most water is desalinated and tastes unpleasant. Drink bottled water (*agua mineral*) sold as *con gaz* (carbonated) and *sin gaz* (still). Drink plenty of water during hot weather.

LANGUAGE

People working in the tourist industry, including waiters, generally know some English. In places where few tourists venture, including bars and restaurants in Arrecife, it is helpful to know some basic Spanish.

Pronunciation guide: *b* almost like a *v*; *c* before *e* or *i* sounds like *th* otherwise like *k*; *d* can be like English *d* or like a *th*; *g* before *e* or *i* is a gutteral *h*, between vowels like *h*, otherwise like *g*; *h* is always silent; *j* gutteral *h*; *ll* like English *lli* (as in million); *ñ* sounds like *ni* in 'onion'; *qu* sound like *k*; *v* sounds a little like *b*; *z* like English *th*.

hotel	*hotel*	breakfast	*el desayuno*
room	*una habitación*	bathroom	*el cuarto de baño*
single/double/	*individual/doble/*	shower	*la ducha*
twin	*con dos camas*	balcony	*el balcón*
one/two nights	*una noche/*	reception	*la recepción*
	dos noches	key	*la llave*
reservation	*una reserva*	room service	*el servicio de habita-*
rate	*la tarifa*		*ciones*

bureau de change	*cambio*	US dollars	*dólares*
post office	*correos*	banknote	*un billete de banco*
ATM	*cajero automático*	travellers' cheques	*cheques de viaje*
foreign exchange	*cambio (de divisas)*	credit card	*la tarjeta de crédito*
foreign currency	*cambio*		
pounds sterling	*la libra esterlina*		

restaurant	*restaurante*	dessert	*el postre*
cafe-bar	*bar*	water	*agua*
table	*una mesa*	(house) wine	*vino (de la casa)*
menu	*la carta*	beer	*cerveza*
set menus	*platos combinados*	drink	*la bebida*
today's set menu	*el plato del día*	bill	*la cuentra*
wine list	*la carta de vinos*	the toilet	*los servicios*
cheers!	*salud!*		

plane	*el avion*	ticket office	*el despacho de billetes*
airport	*el aeropuerto*	timetable	*el horario*
bus	*el autobús ('guagua')*	seat	*un asiento*
ferry	*el ferry*	reserved seat	*un asiento reservado*
terminal	*terminus*		
ticket	*un billete*		
single/return...	*de ida / ...de ida y*		
	vuelta		

yes	*si*	is there..?, do you	*hay...?*
no	*no*	have..?	
please	*por favor*	I don't speak Spanish	*No hablo español*
thank you	*gracias*	I am ...	*Soy ...*
hello/hi	*hola!*	I have ..	*Tengo ...*
hello/good day	*buenos dias*	help!	*socorro!*
sorry/pardon me	*perdon*	how much	*cuánto es?*
bye/see you	*hasta luego*	open	*abierto*
that's fine	*está bien*	closed	*cerrado*
what?	*como?*		

REMEMBER

● Always reconfirm your return flight with the airline or holiday rep at least one day before departing.

● Check in at least 2 hours before the flight departure time.

● Allow time to return your hire car.

Index

TwinPack
Lanzarote & Fuerteventura

Written by   Andrew Sanger
Edited, designed and produced by AA Publishing
Maps   © Automobile Association Developments Limited 2002
Fold-out map   © Freytag-Berndt u. Artaria KG, 1231 Vienna-Austria, all rights reserved

Published and distributed by AA Publishing, a trading name of Automobile Association
Developments Limited, whose registered office is Millstream, Maidenhead Road, Windsor,
Berkshire, SL4 5GD. Registered number 1878835

A CIP catalogue record for this book is available from the British Library.

ISBN 0 7495 3457 5

Colour separation by Chroma Graphics Overseas (PTE) Ltd, Singapore
Printed in Malaysia

ACKNOWLEDGEMENTS
All the pictures used in this publication are held in the Automobile Association's own photo
library (AA Photo Library) and were taken by the following photographers:
ADRIAN BAKER F/Cover (f) palm tree, 49b; STEVE DAY F/Cover (a) Yaiza, volcano, (c) windsurfer,
(e) church, 1, 5b, 6b, 7c, 9, 12t, 12b, 15, 17, 18, 20t, 20b, 21l, 24t, 24b, 25t, 25b, 26b, 29t, 29b,
30t, 30b, 31t, 32t, 32b, 33t, 33b, 34b, 35t, 35b, 36, 37t, 37b, 38t, 38b, 39b, 40t, 40b, 41t, 41b, 44,
46t, 46b, 47, 48, 49t, 50, 51, 52, 53t, 53b, 55, 59, 60, 61b, 84, 85t, 90t, 90bl; ROBERT HOLMES
F/Cover (g) sunbather; CLIVE SAWYER F/Cover (b) strelitzias flower, (d) hiker, bottom sand dunes,
B/Cover camel rider, 5t, 6t, 7t, 7b, 13t, 13b, 14, 16, 19, 21r, 23t, 23b, 26t, 27, 28t, 28b, 31b, 34t,
39t, 42t, 42b, 43t, 43b, 45t, 45b, 56, 58, 61t, 85b, 90br.

Dear **TwinPack** Traveller

**Your comments, opinions and recommendations are very important to us.
So please help us to improve our travel guides by taking a few
minutes to complete this simple questionnaire.**

*You do not need a stamp (unless posted outside the UK). If you do not want to cut this page from your
guide, then photocopy it or write your answers on a plain sheet of paper.*

Send to: **The Editor, AA TwinPack Travel Guides,
FREEPOST SCE 4598, Basingstoke RG21 4GY.**

Your recommendations…

We always encourage readers' recommendations for restaurants, nightlife or shopping – if
your recommendation is used in the next edition of the guide, we will send you a *FREE*
AA TwinPack Guide of your choice. Please state below the establishment name,
location and your reasons for recommending it.

_____

_____

_____

_____

Please send me **AA TwinPack**
 Cyprus ❑ Gran Canaria ❑ Lanzarote & Fuerteventura ❑ Madeira ❑
 Mallorca ❑ Malta & Gozo ❑ Menorca ❑ Tenerife ❑
 (*please tick as appropriate*)

About this guide…

Which title did you buy?
 AA *TwinPack* _____
Where did you buy it? _____
When? m m / y y

Why did you choose an AA *TwinPack* Guide? _____

_____

_____

_____

_____

Did this guide meet your expectations?
 Exceeded ❑ Met all ❑ Met most ❑ Fell below ❑
 Please give your reasons _____

_____

_____

continued on next page…

Were there any aspects of this guide that you particularly liked? _____

_____

_____

_____

Is there anything we could have done better? _____

_____

_____

_____

_____

About you…

Name (*Mr/Mrs/Ms*) _____

Address _____

_____

_____ Postcode _____

Daytime tel no _____

Which age group are you in?

Under 25 ☐   25–34 ☐   35–44 ☐   45–54 ☐   55–64 ☐   65+ ☐

How many trips do you make a year?

Less than one ☐   One ☐   Two ☐   Three or more ☐

Are you an AA member? Yes ☐   No ☐

About your trip…

When did you book? m m / y y   When did you travel? m m / y y

How long did you stay? _____

Was it for business or leisure? _____

Did you buy any other travel guides for your trip?

If yes, which ones? _____

_____

Thank you for taking the time to complete this questionnaire. Please send it to us as soon as

possible, and remember, you do not need a stamp (*unless posted outside the UK*).

Happy Holidays!